The Marionettes

A Linton R. Massey Memorial Publication

William Faulkner
THE MARIONETTES

With an Introduction and Textual Apparatus by
Noel Polk

Published for
The Bibliographical Society
of the University of Virginia
by the University Press of Virginia
Charlottesville

THE UNIVERSITY PRESS OF VIRGINIA
Copyright © 1977 by the Rector and Visitors
of the University of Virginia

This edition first published 1977

Library of Congress Cataloging in Publication Data

Faulkner, William, 1897-1962.
    The Marionettes.

            I. Title.
PS3511.A86M34   1977   812'.5'2   77-8994   ISBN 0-8139-0734-9

Printed in the United States of America

Contents

Acknowledgments	vii
Introduction	ix
The Marionettes	1
Textual Appendixes	
Introduction	79
Descriptions of the Manuscripts	87
Historical Collation	90
Alterations in the Manuscripts	106

Acknowledgments

The Introduction is a revised version of an essay that was originally published as "William Faulkner's *Marionettes*" in the *Mississippi Quarterly*, 26 (Summer 1973), 247–80, and reprinted in James B. Meriwether, ed., *A Faulkner Miscellany* (Jackson, Miss., 1974). I am grateful to Professor Peyton W. Williams, Jr., editor of the *Mississippi Quarterly*, and Barney McKee, Director of the University Press of Mississippi, for permission to use this essay here.

The illustrations from the Texas copies of *The Marionettes*, "Two Puppets in a Fifth Avenue Win[dow]," and the fragmented poem from the early version of *The Marble Faun* are reproduced courtesy of the Humanities Research Center, The University of Texas at Austin, and by the kind permission of Mrs. Paul D. Summers, Jr. I am also grateful to Mr. Howard Duvall for allowing me to examine the Mississippi copy of *Marionettes*.

I wish to thank the literary estate of Roger Fry and the publisher, Chatto & Windus, for permission to quote from *Hérodiade*, from *Stéphane Mallarmé: Poems*, translated by Roger Fry (London, 1936).

Finally, I would like to thank Professor Meriwether for generous assistance and advice at several stages of this work and Professor Morse Peckham for several helpful suggestions about *The Marionettes*. I am very grateful to my wife, Patty, and to Ms. Karen Endres, Prof. Stephen E. Meats, and Ms. Elisabeth S. Muhlenfeld, for their help in collating and proofreading.

Introduction

AMONG THE LONGEST and most ambitious productions of William Faulkner's early career is his one-act play *The Marionettes*, which he wrote, hand-lettered, -decorated, and -bound during his association with the drama group of that name at the University of Mississippi during the fall of 1920. It is a striking, unusual piece, at the same time derivative and original, which obviously occupied a great deal of his time and energy in the writing and extensive revision of the text and in the manner of its "publication." Its facsimile publication in 1975 and particularly its reissue and more general availability in this volume are of special significance to any study of Faulkner's dedication to his craft and his development as an artist in these formative years.[1] One readily sees in it the same rigid artistic discipline that characterizes his later work; it has the tightness of construction and the concentration of effect of the work of the French Symbolist poets, to whom he was going to school; it flatly predicts many of the techniques that were to become so important in his mature work—the structural frame, the counterpointed plot, and diverse viewpoints of the central action—and it even treats a number of themes common to his later fiction: time, change, frustrated sexuality, the relationship between the wilderness and civilization, sterility and fecundity. In short, the germ of much that Faulkner would accomplish during his long and extraordinary career is already present in this apprentice work.

Michael Millgate has suggested that *The Marionettes*' "chief importance" is in its "combination of text with related illustrations and ... its overall stylisation of language, action and line."[2] And though it

---

[1] Two of the four known copies of *The Marionettes* (see Appendix, Introduction) have been published in facsimile: the Virginia copy at Charlottesville, published by the Bibliographical Society of the University of Virginia and the University Press of Virginia in memory of Linton R. Massey, 1975, limited to 126 copies; the Mississippi copy, published at Oxford, the Yoknapatawpha Press, 1975, limited to 510 copies

[2] *The Achievement of William Faulkner* (New York, 1966), p. 8. Besides Millgate, at least four others have drawn attention to *The Marionettes*: James B. Meriwether, *The Literary Career of William Faulkner* (1961; rpt., Columbia, S.C., 1971), pp. 8–9;

Introduction

is difficult to agree that this is its "chief" importance, Faulkner's concern with its physical appearance is very interesting indeed, especially in light of his concern, years later, with the physical appearance of his published work: he specified to Phil Stone, for example, that he wanted *The Marble Faun* bound in "very pale green boards with a straw colored label pasted on the front."[3] The expertise he gained in designing and actually lettering and binding *The Marionettes* (and a series of other pamphlets during the 1920s)[4] puts into a slightly altered perspective his irritation, in 1929, with Ben Wasson's editing of *The Sound and the Fury*: he complained not just that the tampering interfered with the content of the altered passages, but that the printed text, as it stood, presented "a most dull and poorly articulated picture to [his] eye," and he wished that "publishing was advanced enough" for the first section to be printed using different colored inks to indicate time shifts.[5]

The Marionettes is most significant, however, for its purely literary qualities, both for what it tells us about Faulkner's literary concerns at this point in his career and for what it achieves as a work of art in itself. It is a remarkable synthesis of his reading up to that time and is therefore a rich mine for source study. Clearly the work of a young man, it is a showy and self-conscious display of his reading; but it is just as clearly the work of an ambitious and very sophisticated young man who is fully aware of his gift if not yet of his powers; and the display of his reading is so controlled, in its allusions to and borrowings from specific authors, in its deliberate evocation of the mood

---

Carvel Collins, *William Faulkner: Early Prose and Poetry* (Boston, 1962), pp. 11-13, 17-18; James E. Kibler, "William Faulkner and Provincetown Drama, 1920-1922," *Mississippi Quarterly*, 22 (1969), 229, 234-35; and Michel Gresset, "Le regard et le désir chez Faulkner, 1919-1931," *Sud*, No. 14 / 15 (1975), 20-23.

[3] Stone's correspondence with Four Seas, which published *The Marble Faun*, is described and quoted from in the Swann Galleries, Inc., auction catalogue for April 25, 1963, pp. 1-2. These papers are now at the University of Virginia.

[4] Carvel Collins, *Early Prose and Poetry*, pp. 11-13, and *New Orleans Sketches*, (New York, 1968), p. xxx, has called attention to two others, *Mayday* and *The Lilacs*. Joseph Blotner, *Faulkner: A Biography* (New York, 1974), describes a typescript, *Vision in Spring* (pp. 307 ff.), and a holograph sonnet sequence, for which he gives no title (p. 439). I have called attention to *Royal Street: New Orleans* in " 'Hong Li' and *Royal Street*: The New Orleans Sketches in Manuscript," *Mississippi Quarterly*, 26 (1973), 394-95. And according to information supplied with its publication in 1967, a small typescript of *The Wishing Tree* was bound in this manner.

[5] Faulkner to Wasson. Joseph Blotner, ed., *Selected Letters of William Faulkner* (New York, 1977), p. 44.

Introduction

of fin de siècle art and morality, that it becomes an organic part of the whole, a frame of reference, if not quite a controlling metaphor, rather than mere decoration.

Source hunting is at best a chancy business, and when the author is as omnivorous and catholic a reader as Faulkner, the problems are multiplied many times. But there are some obvious starting points for tracing *The Marionettes'* sources, including especially the writers whom Faulkner translated, reviewed, or alluded to in the writing he did for the *Mississippian*, the Ole Miss student newspaper: Verlaine, Mallarmé, Swinburne, Wilde, Housman, Millay, O'Neill, and others.[6] Carvel Collins suggests the influence of Amy Lowell's "Patterns" on the play, and Millgate believes that the Beardsley-illustrated edition of Oscar Wilde's *Salomé*, which was in Faulkner's library at the time of his death, may have been at least one source for its "stylisation and vague, *fin de siècle* sensuality."[7] It is, as will be seen, the source for much more than that. Wilde's short poem "The Harlot's House" seems to be part of the general background of *The Marionettes*, as is the poetry of T. S. Eliot, especially "The Love Song of J. Alfred Prufrock," which is paraphrased several times in the play, as well as throughout Faulkner's poetry, published and unpublished. Marietta's "awakening" and her fondness for her own image in the pool may owe something to Eve's awakening in Book IV of *Paradise Lost*. The most pervasive influence, however, seems to have been that of the French Symbolists: not only Verlaine and Mallarmé, but also Laforgue, Huysmans, Baudelaire, Gourmont, Valéry, Gautier, and Flaubert, to name only a few, whom he seems to have been reading at the time.[8]

---

[6] Richard P. Adams, in the first chapter, "Apprenticeship," of his *Faulkner: Myth and Motion* (Princeton, 1968), and Margaret Yonce, in her *"Soldiers' Pay:* A Critical Study of William Faulkner's First Novel," Diss. South Carolina 1970, offer particularly useful discussions of influences on Faulkner's early work. See also Cleanth Brooks, "Faulkner as Poet," *Southern Literary Journal*, 1 (Dec. 1968), 5-19; Addison C. Bross, *"Soldiers' Pay* and the Art of Aubrey Beardsley," *American Quarterly*, 19 (1967), 3-23; H. Edward Richardson, "The Decadence in Faulkner's Frist [sic] Novel: The Faun, the Worm, and the Tower," *Etudes Anglaises*, 21 (1968), 225-35; and M. Gidley, "One Continuous Force: Notes on Faulkner's Extra-Literary Reading," *Mississippi Quarterly*, 23 (1970), 299-314.

[7] *Early Prose and Poetry*, p. 18; Millgate, pp. 8-9.

[8] Collins, for example, *Early Prose and Poetry*, p. 13, says that Faulkner "imported" the French Symbolists to the University of Mississippi campus, and even though for many of these writers I can find no specific indebtedness, the general mood and tone of their works make it evident that Faulkner was reading them—and others—heavily.

Introduction

Faulkner translated, or adapted, for the *Mississippian*, four poems by Paul Verlaine.[9] Two of them, "Fantoches" and "Clair de Lune," are specifically related to *The Marionettes*. In "Fantoches," the French word for "Puppets," commedia dell'arte characters play out their lives in the light of a cold and passionless moon, which watches without the slightest concern for human affairs: "la lune ne garde aucune rancune," as Faulkner describes it in a line borrowed not from Verlaine but from Jules Laforgue's "Complainte de cette bonne lune," perhaps through Eliot's paraphrase in his "Rhapsody on a Windy Night."[10] "Clair de Lune" is practically an outline of *The Marionettes*: it is set in a garden where masquers dance and sing in vain attempts to hide from themselves the sadness of their lives, while the moon, again calm, passionless, and eternal, looks on in splendid ironical contrast:

> Your soul is a lovely garden, and go
> There masque and bergamasque charmingly,
> Playing the lute and dancing and also
> Sad beneath their disguising [fantasy].[11]
>
> All are singing in a minor key
> Of conqueror love and life opportune,
> Yet seem to doubt their joyous revelry
> As their song melts in the light of the moon.
>
> In the calm moonlight, so lovely fair
> That makes the birds dream in the slender trees,
> While fountains dream among the statues there;
> Slim fountains sob in silver ecstasies.

Finally, one important if somewhat surprising source for *The Marionettes* is almost certainly a play by Laurence Housman and H. Granville-Barker entitled *Prunella, or Love in a Dutch Garden*, published in 1906. There is no direct evidence that Faulkner knew it, beyond its numerous striking parallels with *The Marionettes*, though either drama critic and novelist Stark Young or Phil Stone could have made it available to him. The action of *Prunella*, like that of *The Marionettes*, takes place in a highly formal garden, hedged by a fence, with a fountain in the middle. Like Marietta, Prunella is the illegitimate child of

---

[9] Collected in *Early Prose and Poetry*: "Fantoches," p. 57; "Clair de Lune," p. 58; "Streets," p. 59, and "A Clymène," p. 61.

[10] Adams's suggestion, p. 39.

[11] I have adopted Collins's suggestion, *Early Prose and Poetry*, p. 128, that "fantasy," instead of the apparently misprinted "fanchise," is the correct word here.

Introduction

a mother who has been seduced and abandoned; both (like Quentin Compson, some years later) have been returned by their mothers to the very homes from which they themselves had fled; both are reared by three maiden aunts: Prunella's are named Prim, Prude, and Privacy; Marietta's are unnamed, but they are called "three grey aunts! / Three drab grey moths" (p. 23). Both Marietta and Prunella are enticed away from the garden by a lothario named Pierrot, and both gardens go to ruin when they are taken away. Both Pierrots claim kinship with the moon: Prunella's lover tells her he is the man in the moon, and Marietta's sings that the moon is his "foster mother in the sky" (p. 27). Even though, then, *Prunella* is for the most part a fluffy and insubstantial romantic comedy in which Prunella and Pierrot are happily reunited after their trials, whereas in *The Marionettes* they are not, it seems clear that *Prunella* stands significantly in the background of Faulkner's play.

I

The Marionettes opens with a description of the stage setting, which establishes a pervasive tone of formality and artificiality, and introduces a number of the more important symbols:

> The sky is a thin transparent blue, a very light blue merging into white with stars in regular order, and a full moon. At the back center is a marble colonnade, small in distance, against a regular black band of trees; on either side of it is the slim graceful silhouette of a single poplar tree. Both wings are closed by sections of wall covered with roses, motionless on the left wall is a peacock silhouetted against the moon. In the middle fore ground is a pool and a fountain. [Pp. 1-2]

The second paragraph is a description of the accompanying drawing—though it will doubtless be noted that there is no mandolin in any of the copies of this drawing, just as there is a full moon only in the Virginia copy; nor is there, though the second paragraph describes it, a scarf of black and gold Chinese brocade draped across Pierrot's chair—which introduces us to the dissipated major character, Pierrot, whose physical and apparently emotional disorder is juxtaposed with the "regular order" of the stars and the "regular" trees:

Introduction

Pierrot is seated at right front in a fragile black chair beside a delicate table. His left arm is curved across the table top, his right arm hangs beside him, and his head rests upon his curved arm, face toward front. He appears to be in a drunken sleep, there is a bottle and an overtunned wine glass upon the table, a mandoline and a woman's slipper lie at his feet. He does not change his position during the play. He is dressed in white and black. Flung across the chair back is a scarf of black and gold Chinese brocade. [Pp. 2–3]

The statement that he "does not change his position during the play" is structurally very important, and in the later, revised, texts of *The Marionettes*, Faulkner stressed its importance by placing it as the final sentence of the paragraph.[12] It draws our attention immediately and somewhat enigmatically back to the list of "Persons" in the play, which lists not just "Pierrot" but "Shade of Pierrot" as well. Thus the drunken clown Pierrot, onstage throughout, seems to be the operative figure in the play, and the implication is that the action of the play takes place in Pierrot's head, either as a dream of himself as the would-be lover, like Mallarmé's and Faulkner's fauns, or as a guilt-ridden dream of remorse over what he has done to Marietta.

The stage set, the two principal commentators, who appear at each important juncture in the play, enter; called the Grey Figure and the Lilac Figure in the list of Persons, they are identified when they speak only as "First Figure" and "Second Figure." They enter in a "slightly unnatural rythm" (p. 3), which suggests both their kinship to Pierrot— they are his servants—and their alienage in the formal atmosphere of the garden; paradoxically, their speeches are highly formal and ornate, and filled with elaborate similes, like those of the Page of Herodias and the Young Syrian in the opening scene of Wilde's *Salomé*. The First Figure calls attention to the stillness in the garden: "How still it is! The air does not stir, the air is like a candle flaming in a dusky colonnade" (p. 4); but the Second Figure argues that it is not still: "The sky is like a blue candle flame," he says, "the sky is a curtain of thin blue silk, and the wind stirs it gently like a white hand" (p. 4).

It soon becomes clear, however, that their disagreement has nothing really to do with whether the wind is blowing, but with their differing ways of perceiving and responding to the world; here the response is to the garden, later it will be to Marietta and her changed circumstances. The First Figure appears to see only the externalities, the rigid formality and artificiality of the garden, and his speeches are filled with harsh images, of death and violence, which reinforce his

---

[12] See the Historical Collation at the end of this volume.

Introduction

vision of the garden world as sterile and unlovely: "The moon is like a dismembered breast upon the floor of a silent sea," he says; "the moon is like the bloated face of a scorned woman who has drowned her self. How still it is!" (p. 6). The Second Figure, however, seems to understand that it is, after all, a garden, and that underneath all the cold and clipped rigidity things do live and die; his speeches, consequently, are filled with images of life and art: the twin poplars are for him "like two blind virgins" that "sway in unison like two violin bows," and even the nine columns of the colonnade are for him "nine muses standing like votive candles before a blue mountain" (pp. 6–7); to the First Figure they are like "*statues* of virgins in dark green bronze," whose shadows are unreal and dimensionless like "reflections of two candles in a flat mirror" (p. 8; emphasis supplied).

The point of their discussion, the larger problem, is the paradox which the formal garden represents: that is, to what extent can nature be so carefully ordered and controlled and still be nature, perpetuating life? To what extent can an individual submit to any of civilization's rules and still remain free? Absolute freedom can only result in anarchy and chaos—witness Nancy Mannigoe's disregard of the law, Charlotte Rittenmeyer's disregard of convention, and Temple Drake's disregard of both—and so it is essential that society enforce certain rules of behavior: but at what point do those rules, controls, actually destroy the life they were meant to nurture and sustain? It is one of the major themes of Faulkner's great fiction—*Go Down, Moses*, for example, and *Requiem for a Nun*—in which the wilderness and the community are central metaphors for freedom and bondage, and it is significant to see him working with it at the beginning of his career, even though on a much smaller scale.

The formal garden, then, is the underlying symbol of *The Marionettes*, and the extended contrasting descriptions of it in the first few pages draw our attention to the kinship between the garden and Marietta, the soon-to-be-betrayed. One scene in *Prunella* specifically defines the symbolic function of the garden there; the definition applies to *The Marionettes* as well. Prunella, hidden from the outside world behind a high wall, enters the stage preparing for her "lessons," a daily recitation of the aphorisms of modest living, which her aunts require of her. She encounters a gardener at work clipping the hedge:

PRUNELLA. What are you doing there?
3RD GAR. Giving Nature a lesson, miss.
PRUNELLA. What are you teaching her?

Introduction

3RD GAR. To keep straight! I'll let her know who's master while *I'm* here.
PRUNELLA. And if you didn't, what would happen?
3RD GAR. Why, she'd kick over the traces and be off her own way in no time. She's bad enough as it is, always getting herself [*clips*] out of shape, and trying to be different to what you make her. [*Clips.*] Well, that you can't help, you've just got to come along and put it right. [*Clips.*] First she'll run to leaf—that you can't help—then she'll run to seed—that you can't help—then she goes stalky [*clips*] rots herself—dies and stinks. None of it you can't help.
PRUNELLA. What can you do, then?
3RD GAR. Oh, you—you—can make things uncomfortable for her; you can show her what she ought to be, and keep her in her place—make her toe the line. That's what a garden's for, that's where gardening comes in.[13]

Thus the purpose of the garden is to bridle nature, to control it; the purpose of "instruction" is to bridle human nature, to teach it to control itself. Too much control, however, is just as bad as too little, since either creates an imbalance between freedom and restraint that throws both nature and civilization into chaos: consider Zilphia Gant, Howard Boyd, and Temple Drake, for example. Likewise, it is the overprotection of Prunella and Marietta, by their well-intentioned aunts, that renders them unable to cope with the devices of a scoundrel like Pierrot.

One thinks immediately of at least two other formal gardens in Faulkner's work: that of the marble faun, who is totally incapable of giving way to his passions, though he longs to, and of the formal garden in *Soldiers' Pay*, which forms such an important part of the symbolic structure of that novel. Margaret Yonce suggests that the garden's "very formality serves a symbolic function by placing it outside the ordinary realm of activity"; but it also symbolizes the restrictive controls which Reverend Mahon, who designed it, and Margaret Powers, who loves to walk in it, have put over their own emotional lives—Reverend Mahon, who "has withdrawn into his garden where life flows about him without affecting him," and Mrs. Powers, who is not able to give herself completely, for many different reasons, to anyone.[14] It is also significant that Narcissa Benbow Sartoris, perhaps the coldest, most aloof, and most destructive of Faulkner's women—in her very narcissism and her capacities for destruction she is a direct descendant of Marietta—is so frequently seen working in a garden in *Flags in the Dust* and *Sanctuary*. By way of contrast it is worth noting

---
[13] *Prunella*, pp. 11-12.
[14] Yonce, pp. 48, 52. Her complete discussion of the garden covers pp. 47-49.

Introduction

that in his unfinished novel *Elmer*, written about the time of *Soldiers' Pay*, Faulkner described Paris, that Western symbol for all that is voluptuous and sensual and unrestrained, as a "homely *informal* garden."[15] Significantly, Pierrot claims to have been born "In Paris town" (pp. 14–15).

Like the garden, then, Marietta displays a cold and formal exterior which has been developed and nurtured by her "three grey aunts," who want to keep her from making the same mistake her mother had made; Marietta, as a result, is actually seething with an urge, specifically sexual, which she can neither fully understand nor cope with. She enters dressed in white, but before speaking she makes three symbolic gestures: she pauses at the fountain, invoking the image of Narcissus, with which she is to be associated throughout the play; she then "faces the moon and lifts her arms with a sudden gesture" (p. 9), making obeisance to all of the moon's paradoxical meanings: symbol of love and beauty, symbol of the chaste and sterile, but beautiful, huntress, and symbol of the insignificance of man in the eyes of the powers that control the world: la lune ne garde aucune rancune. Finally, she "goes over to the rose bush at left and draws a great armful of them about her face" (p. 9), a gesture that might be interpreted as her identification with nature, an expression of the healthiness of her sexual urges; but it is also possible that the roses are for her primarily self-decoration, to be contrasted with the gaudier jewels and clothing she is to ornament herself with in the latter part of the play. Doubtless Faulkner intended the contrasting images of the artificial and the natural to suggest, even at this point in the play, ambivalence in her character.

This ambivalence is nicely symbolized by the disparity between the mechanical formality of her diction and her movements on stage — when speaking she stands, like a marionette, "in a slightly strained but graceful attitude" (p. 10) — and the emotional intensity her actual words express. Several things are worth noting in her speech (pp. 10–14). First is her anxiety, her "strange desires" for "vague, unnamed things," which she traces directly to her "narrow bed" (p. 10), a phrase Faulkner borrows from his own adaptation of Verlaine's "Fantoches," in which the half-naked daughter of the doctor of Bogona "Glides trembling from her narrow bed" for a sexual tryst with her "lover waiting in the moon."[16] The "singing voice" (p. 11) which disturbs her

---
[15] Quoted in Millgate, p. 21 (my italics).
[16] *Early Prose and Poetry*, p. 57.

is clearly the voice of her own emotions, long repressed; the nightingales, which apparently are related to those "melodious but slightly tiresome nightingales in a formal clipped hedge" that Faulkner referred to a couple of years later,[17] have fled (p. 11), as Marietta flees, from that emotion: that is, Marietta's anxiety is caused by the tension between her felt need to enter the world of experience and her fear of the unknown. "Am I afraid of a darkened room?" she wonders (p. 11). The honeysuckle, as it is to Quentin Compson nearly a decade later, is a stimulus, urging on her sexuality (p. 12), and her body, like Dewey Dell Bundren's, is "hot like the earth of a noon drenched garden" (p. 13) and in direct conflict with the emotionless garden. Significantly, she suppresses her anxieties in the pool, cools her ardor in another narcissistic gesture—"She approaches the pool . . . slips off her gown and steps slowly into the water" (p. 14)—which anticipates her sterile immersion in herself in the final scene.

While she is "cooling" herself, the singing voice which "disturbed [her] dreams" (p. 10), which filled her with "strange desires," becomes audible; it is the voice of Pierrot, or the "Shade of Pierrot," apparently, and a chorus, singing just over the wall. Their song (pp. 14–18) is not much as poetry, but it is appropriate to both the play and Pierrot, very rhythmic and spirited, and well-suited to the character of the marionette whom one imagines dancing, in counterfeited liveliness, to pulled strings on the other side of the wall. "O fair sweet maid," they sing to Marietta, "come dance with us!" (p. 18).

Pierrot is, then, the incarnation of Marietta's unconscious desires. He identifies himself with the moon, to which Marietta has just offered supplication, and by injecting himself and the "high dissonnance" (p. 16) of his mandolin into the garden, he threatens to disturb its stately formality; by injecting passion into Marietta's waking consciousness, he threatens to disturb the cool and safe regularity of her life. Leaping upon the wall, he sings directly to her: "You are a trembling pool," he croons, "And I am a flame that only you can quench. . . . Let me drown myself between your breast points, / Beloved" (pp. 20–21).

Marietta listens, "frightened," and makes the formal gesture of clasping her hands across her breast (p. 22), even though, apparently, she is still in the water, still naked, and "hypnotised" by Pierrot. Confronted so directly by her desires, she retreats instinctively to the security which order has given her life up till now, and her reply,

[17] "American Drama: Inhibitions," *Early Prose and Poetry*, p. 95.

Introduction

unlike the impassioned, anxious prose of her opening speech, is in very clipped and formal and controlled iambic tetrameter couplets (pp. 22–23). Her refusal is so formal and deliberate as to seem almost by rote, and there is a sense in which she is perhaps merely going through the motions, while actually planning to accept. She is finally, rather easily, convinced, and after a single refusal she accepts Pierrot's invitation. He tells her to come "without regretting" (p. 26); as she reaches the wall he lifts her up, and, like the puppets Scaramouche and Pulcinella in Verlaine's "Fantoches"—but not in Faulkner's adaptation of it—they make a "single black silhouette against the moon" (p. 26), ominously, as if to emphasize the sterility of the relationship they are embarking upon: la lune ne garde aucune rancune indeed. They leave together, to the fading sound of Pierrot's song of conquest (pp. 27–28).

Immediately the scene changes: the moon "disappears behind a cloud, leaving the stage in darkness"; the Grey and Lilac figures are seen "dimly" on stage, and, to the accompaniment of the "low tones of a violin" (pp. 28–29), they discuss the sudden change of season. "It is sudden cold," the First Figure says; he notes the dying trees and then announces that the "Spirit of Autumn" is in the garden. The Second Figure's response has significance that will only become clear later in the play: "Yes," he says, "the leaves are dying. All things must die, and dead things are very heavy" (pp. 29–30).

II

The interlude that follows is the most distinctive structural feature of *The Marionettes*. It specifically anticipates one of Faulkner's favorite fictional devices, the bold insertion into a work of an episode either slightly digressive from the main narrative, like the horse thief episode in *A Fable*, or completely divorced from it, like the "Old Man" sections of *The Wild Palms*, which serves as a thematic counterpoint to the main plot. The episode here parallels the story of Pierrot and Marietta and by implication anticipates the unhappy ending to their affair; it is an allegory in which a garden nymph, thriving in her garden's fullness, her breasts "like two birds in the shadow of her hair" and her "long fair hair [hanging] down and the moon . . .

Introduction

combed through it like spun silver" (p. 32), is abandoned by her lover, a personified "Summer"—abandoned as Marietta is to be abandoned.

It is a fable of the seasons, and, narrated by the Spirit of Autumn, the image and spirit of mortality, is rife with the sense of the necessity of change and the inevitability of death.[18] The Spirit of Autumn does not attribute their parting to any kind of dissatisfaction with each other—"They have not quarrelled," he insists, "I am sure the[y] have not quarrelled" (p. 32)—but only to the workings of time. Summer in fact challenges, briefly, the mechanism of change; when he hears the nymph's voice calling after him he stops, "half turned toward her," and "for a fleeting second he is the utter master of his soul; Fate and the gods stand aloof, watching him, his destiny waits wordless on either hand." But even though his freedom is in his grasp, "he goes on," unable to resist his destiny, "his young eyes ever before him, looking into the implacable future" (p. 34).

It is also more than a fable of the seasons, for the Spirit of Autumn's commentary invests it with a significance directly related to the story of Pierrot and Marietta and with even broader significance for Faulkner's later works. The Spirit of Autumn suggests reasons for Summer's refusal to return to the garden: "Perhaps a newer, stronger love has called him away, perhaps he is fallen upon by wild beasts while traversing a dark forest, or perhaps, while crossing a stream, he slipped and was drowned" (pp. 34-35). The "newer, *stronger* love" is not clearly identified, but the suggestion, given the allegory, is that death itself, Summer's own inexorable movement toward autumn, "has called him away." There are at least two reasons to think this: first, it anticipates Marietta's statement, when she returns, that "nothing save death" is as beautiful as she is; second, and related to it, is the suggestion of Summer's narcissistic death by drowning: one immediately thinks of Bayard Sartoris and, as Carvel Collins has pointed out, Quentin Compson, both of whom destroy themselves, Quentin specifically by drowning, with their constant immersion in themselves.[19] The most important implication, however, is the fatalistic pall cast over the entire play by the fact that it is Summer, the very life force itself, which is in love with death.

The remainder of the Spirit of Autumn's narrative confirms this

---

[18] Both Millgate, p. 8, and Collins, *Early Prose and Poetry*, p. 18, suggest that the episode, narrated by the Spirit of Autumn, is about Pierrot and Marietta; but it is so only by implication.

[19] *Early Prose and Poetry*, p. 18.

Introduction

view of the interlude. The garden nymph now "waits in vain" for Summer's return in the dead garden, "among her dried rose stalks" (p. 35). Her "warning of disaster had been a true warning," he says, "the disaster had come to pass" (p. 36). He then repeats the refrain of the song she had sung when Summer left, when she had sent "her heart after him across the sweet pagan heart break of the September night" (pp. 32–33), but which now is much more poignant and thematically significant: "Though ever love call and call / He will not hear at all" (p. 36). The Spirit of Autumn then explains: "no matter what faces bend above him or what mouths sing to his unheeding ears" (p. 36), he will not respond to the forces of life. In his total concern for himself, his constant seeking for new sensations, self-satisfaction—his love of death—Summer has cut himself off from love. The episode ends with an image of the moon as Narcissus which more than anything else defines the meaning of the symbol of the moon in the play. The garden nymph sits alone with her sorrow, while the "half moon in the sky is forever staring blank face to blank face with the half moon in the stream" (p. 36). Indeed, yet again, la lune ne garde aucune rancune.

III

The garden to which Marietta returns is dead, and is dominated by the Spirit of Autumn, who remains silently on the wall during the play's final scene, supplying a "background in a single tone against which the succeeding action takes place" (p. 37); the remaining action is imbued with the imminence of death.

Marietta is preceded on stage by the Grey and Lilac figures, who discuss the autumnal setting: "This garden is old," the First Figure says; "the earth is already old, the earth is like an aged woman gathering fagots in a barren field" (p. 38). The Second Figure agrees: "Hither come the ghosts of stripped springs grown cold and dumb and sightless . . . the hills are bare of any life" (p. 39). Age, sterility, and death: the birds are gone, the trees are bare, the grey autumn sky is reflected narcissistically in the pool (pp. 40–41), and "the passing days scatter like petals on the ground" (p. 40), the First Figure says. The Second Figure responds with two significant images. The first is directly related to "Study," a poem Faulkner wrote at about this time and published in the *Mississippian*, in which a student whose every sense is responding to the burgeoning spring world outside his classroom window wishes that he "were a bust / All head" so that he can concentrate more completely on his studies.[20] In *The Marionettes* the image is applied directly to the statues in the garden, which "are not cold" because they "are all head" (p. 41). They are fit inhabitants of such a garden, then, precisely because they are lifeless; the body has been suppressed by an act of the mind, which is what Marietta, upon returning, will have done to herself. The Second Figure's other comment is an image of death that stands in direct complement to the Spirit of Autumn's closing image of the moon as Narcissus: "The leaves shake from the blond boughs and slide down the sky hill, and the moon, even the moon is a dead leaf blown across the sky" (p. 41).

Under this dead narcissistic moon, with the Spirit of Autumn dominating the background, Marietta reappears, completely changed, at least externally. Wearing a "flame colored gown" instead of the white gown she wore on her first appearance, she "comes to the front looking about her as if she had never seen the garden before" (p. 42). She is apprehensive at the changes, both in the garden and in herself: "How this garden has changed!" she observes. "Why has it changed so? Ah, [I] know, it is autumn that has changed the garden. But I am not changed. Am I changed very much, I wonder! (p. 42). As before, she suppresses her emotional agitation by looking at her reflection in the pool (pp. 42–43).

While she studies her own image, the Grey and Lilac figures, who hid themselves when she reappeared, begin to discuss her, and in their reactions to her at this point they cease being merely chorus and become characters in their own right; their comments add an important if minor thematic dimension to the play. For in the beginning the reader tends to react negatively to the First Figure, who described the garden in the opening scene with images of death and dismemberment, and rather more favorably to the Second Figure who, at least apparently, saw life there. During this final exchange, however, it becomes clear that our initial impressions of them are wrong; for here both agree that Marietta is beautiful (pp. 43–44), even though they describe her in completely different terms. The Second Figure admires her only as one admires an objet d'art: "She is like an ivory tower built by black slaves, and surrounded by flames, she is like a

[20] Ibid., pp. 62–63.

little statue of ivory and silver for which blood has been spilt" (p. 43); her hair is "gold, it is as gold as a galleon captured by pirates, gold bleachened with blood and passion" (p. 44); "her eyes are like pools in which one could drown oneself, her breast is a narrow white pool, and her breast points are the twin reflections of stars. Her breasts are like ivory crusted jewels for which men have died, for which armies have slain one another and brother has has [sic] murdered brother" (pp. 45-46). That is, she is beautiful to him because of her gaudy artificiality, because of the aura of death and violence which she emanates. Thus his earlier pleasure in the garden was not at all in his response to natural beauty, as it seemed, but in his admiration of its clipped and combed, cool and regular formality; he responds to art as he does not respond to life.

The First Figure, however, who saw only death in the garden, now sees a very fragile Marietta; she is to him "like a slender birch tree stripped by a storm, she is a birch tree shivering at dawn upon a dim wood; no, she is like a young poplar between a white river and a road" (pp. 43-44);[21] her hair "is like the sun upon a field of wheat, it is like sunlight combed through maple leaves" (p. 44). He disliked the garden, then, because he saw it as too restrictive of nature, and therefore life-denying; by the same token he understands Marietta, under all the decoration, to be a vulnerable, and hurt, human being. He responds more directly to life than to art, and he would seem to be the healthier, the more nearly normal, of the two figures.

The point is not unimportant, for Faulkner seems here to be making a comment about art that has some significance for his own career: it is not difficult to see in the Second Figure Faulkner's implicit criticism of the so-called art-for-art's-sake movement, with its emphasis on and sterile contemplation of form, color, and control, a kind of narcissism in itself, which denied that life had any real meaning outside of art. Michael Millgate has well said that "Faulkner's major concerns, like those of all great artists, were ultimately moral, and there is little value in abstract discussions of his ideas which fail to take this into account," and Faulkner is here, even this early in his career, at least indirectly voicing that moral concern with the problems of being human that is at the root of all his mature writing.[22]

At any rate, their discussion of Marietta forms a fine choral coun-

---

[21] Faulkner also used this phrase in "A Poplar," *Early Prose and Poetry*, p. 60.
[22] Millgate, p. 287.

terpoint to her own comments as she stares at herself in the pool: "I have not changed, I am really beautiful now" (p. 43). Both figures seem to be right about her: she is a vulnerable, terribly wounded character, and though she has changed externally, like the garden itself, she is still the same person she has always been. We are asked to believe her when she says that she is not changed, and to reinterpret her earlier actions in light of the way we see her now. Indeed, she has been constantly associated with images of vanity and pride throughout, especially the peacocks and the narcissistic pool; these come to a point here and in her long closing speech, in which she defines her character most directly. The implication is that she has been a vain and sterile character, at least potentially, from the beginning; and, possibly, that she succumbed to Pierrot not just because of his romantic allure but simply because he was paying attention to her, flattering her vanity—just as Narcissa Benbow, in *Flags in the Dust*, refuses to destroy Byron Snopes's amatory letters, which simultaneously appall and stimulate her, because in them she has concrete evidence that she is the object of somebody's desire. There is also the real possibility, since we are given only indirect evidence to the contrary—that is, we are not specifically told what happens between Marietta and Pierrot after they leave the garden—that it is Marietta who has in fact deserted Pierrot, broken his heart, as it were, after having recognized in herself the power to do so, and left him to waste himself away in dissipation, rather than the other way around, as we are led to believe by the Spirit of Autumn's narrative of Summer and the garden nymph. This would certainly be consistent with her character as we now perceive her, and it would suggest other dimensions to the reasons for Pierrot's onstage drunkenness.

Marietta's final speech (pp. 48–55), which also ends the play, is a long and intricately developed peroration that sums up and restates many of the play's themes. It is a speech full of vanity and pride. Her repeated emphasis on weight and heaviness—her hair so "heavy with gold" that it will hurt her head (p. 49)—recalls the Second Figure's earlier comment that "dead things are very heavy" (p. 30), and the image of her breasts as "twin moons that have been dead for a thousand years, [staring] heavily over [her] girdle" (p. 53) evokes the First Figure's description of the moon as "a dismembered breast upon the floor of a silent sea," as "the bloated face of a scorned woman who has drowned herself" (p. 6). The accreting images of death, vanity, and narcissism culminate in the fine wasteland symbol of the "grey," ashy

Introduction

ilex surrounding the marble-bound Hermes (pp. 51-52); the play ends with the highly suggestive image of the cold and sterile moon's "playing" Marietta's cold and sterile body, and with the information that the ilex has been "blighted" by the "cacophonous cries" (pp. 54-55)—like the "high dissonnance" of Pierrot's mandolin—of the vain and voluptuous peacocks: all together reinforce the play's theme that narcissism is, finally, a form of death.

The statue of Hermes, which is not mentioned until Marietta's return, is the central symbol of Marietta's speech and may well be the central symbol of the entire play. For Hermes was, of course, among the most mobile of the Greek gods, and certainly one of the most virile, wooing and winning the sexual favors of goddesses and mortals alike. He was a lover of Aphrodite, the goddess of fertility; and he was the father of Pan, the original faun. He invented the reed pipe, so closely connected with Pan, and the lyre, which Faulkner surely intends us to associate with Pierrot's mandolin. Further, Hermes was traditionally represented as a bust atop a herm, which was adorned with a phallus. Marietta's garden has become a wintry wasteland where life itself has been stifled, marble-bound. This seems to be no less true of Marietta than of Pierrot, both of whom will, like the marble faun in Faulkner's first book, and by implication like the statue of Hermes, watch the world change and grow, without being able to participate in the change and growth. Faulkner may or may not have known, finally, that one of the scandals of the Greek world was the mutilation of the numerous statues of Hermes in Athens.[23] If he did (and there is no phallus on the statue of Hermes in the illustration facing page 32, though certainly that may be without meaning), the emasculated Hermes, a "bust all head" and no body at all, surrounded by the "blighted" ilex, becomes an even more specific symbol of the dissipated Pierrot, lying in a drunken sleep on one side of the stage, who in his very excesses is destroying the life that is in him.

No less than Hermes is Marietta divorced from her body, from the procreative part of herself that must change or die, and in this way she emerges at the end of the play as type and symbol, perhaps even twentieth-century avatar, of a kind of woman who appears frequently in European literature of the late nineteenth century—Gautier's Cleo-

---

[23] Michael Avi Yonah and Israel Shatzman, *Illustrated Encyclopaedia of the Classical World* (New York, 1975), p. 232; Sir Paul Harvey, comp. and ed., *The Oxford Companion to Classical Literature* (Oxford, 1940), p. 204.

Introduction

patra and Flaubert's Salammbô, for example.[24] In particular Faulkner is alluding to and borrowing from Wilde's *Salomé* and Mallarmé's *Hérodiade*, both portraits of such women.

It has already been suggested that the dialogue between the Grey and Lilac figures is in the manner of the opening speeches of *Salomé*; but Faulkner also borrows more directly from Wilde's highly stylized drama. Herod, for example, in trying to dissuade Salomé from having the head of Jokanaan, offers her, first, his "beautiful white peacocks," which bear a remarkable resemblance to those Marietta describes: "Their beaks are gilded with gold," he tells Salomé, "and the grains that they eat are gilded with gold also, and their feet are stained with purple. When they cry out the rain comes, and the moon shows herself in the heavens when they spread their tails." That failing, Herod offers her jewels

> that are marvellous. I have a collar of pearls, set in four rows. They are like unto moons chained with rays of silver. They are like fifty moons caught in a golden net. On the ivory of her breast a queen has worn it. Thou shalt be as fair as a queen when thou wearest it. I have amethysts of two kinds, one that is black like wine, and one that is red like wine which has been coloured with water. I have topazes, yellow as are the eyes of tigers, and topazes that are pink as the eyes of a wood-pigeon, and green topazes that are as the eyes of cats. I have opals that burn always, with an icelike flame, opals that make sad men's minds, and are fearful of the shadows. I have onyxes like the eyeballs of a dead woman.

More important, however, is the pervasive image of the moon throughout the play. Like Marietta, Salomé makes obeisance to it when she first appears:

> How good to see the moon! She is like a little piece of money, you would think she was a little silver flower. The moon is cold and chaste. I am sure she is a virgin, she has a virgin's beauty. Yes, she is a virgin. She has never defiled herself. She has never abandoned herself to men, like the other goddesses.

And when Salomé insists upon having Jokanaan brought before her, the Page of Herodias says, "Oh! How strange the moon looks. You would think it was the hand of a dead woman who is seeking to cover herself with a shroud."[25] Marietta is, of course, fully capable of Salomé's cruelty; this is implicit both in the Second Figure's descrip-

---

[24] See the chapter entitled "Byzantium" in Mario Praz, *The Romantic Agony*, trans. Angus Davidson, 2d ed. (London, 1970), for a thorough discussion of the background of this type of woman.

[25] *The Works of Oscar Wilde* (London, 1906), pp. 199, 60, 10-11, 16.

Introduction

tion of her and in the image of voracity in Marietta's description of her peacock's eyes as "like the eyes of wolves upon a wood's edge," as becoming "avid and thick and remorseless as the eyes of virgins growing old" (pp. 50, 53).

The most specific borrowing, however, seems to be from Mallarmé's *Hérodiade*. "Hérodiade," suggests Wallace Fowlie, "is a soul seeking to escape from the state of becoming"; she "opposes the flow and the change of life by her studied and concentrated frigidity."[26] Like Marietta, the heroine of Mallarmé's poem is enamored of the "blonde torrent of [her] immaculate hair" and tells her attendant nurse that her hairs "are not flowers / To spread forgetfulness of human ills, / But gold." Also like Marietta, Hérodiade equates beauty and death; and, looking into a mirror, which she addresses as "A cold water frozen with ennui," she wonders "am I beautiful?" Her attendant, very disturbed by her unwillingness to love, asks her for whom she is keeping herself; Hérodiade's reply is almost a gloss on Marietta's final soliloquy:

H[érodiade]. For myself.
N[urse]. Sad flower which grows alone and has no other joy
    Than its own image seen in water listlessly.
      . . . . .
H. Besides, I want naught human, and if sculptured
    You see me with eyes lost in Paradise
    'Tis when I bring to mind your milk once drunk.
N. Ah! Lamentable victim offered to its fate!
H. Yes, it's for me, for me that I flower, deserted!
    You know it, gardens of amethyst, hid
    Endlessly in cunning abysses and dazzled,
    Ignored gold, keeping your antique light
    Under the sombre sleep of a primaeval soil,
    You stones whence my eyes like pure jewels
    Borrow their melodious brightness, and you
    Metals which give my youthful tresses
    A fatal splendour and their massive sway![27]

Marietta, then, has direct literary connections with the life-denying, life-destroying fatal woman of late nineteenth-century literature; so too does Pierrot have literary ancestors other than the

---

[26] *Mallarmé* (Chicago, 1953), p. 127. This is a book of interest to all Faulknerians, especially the chapter on "L'Après-Midi d'un Faune."
[27] *Stéphane Mallarmé: Poems*, trans. Roger Fry (London, 1936), pp. 79, 81, 83, 85.

harlequins and pagliaccis of the commedia dell'arte tradition. If on the one hand the play is the drunken Pierrot's guilt-ridden dream of remorse, he is, like Januarius Jones in *Soldiers' Pay*, at least a collateral descendant of James Branch Cabell's Jurgen, whose "indiscriminate lechery" always leaves him unsatiated, unsatisfied, and unfulfilled.[28] If on the other hand the play is Pierrot's fantasy, a dream of himself as the all-conquering, irresistible lover, then he is directly descended from the frustrated faun in Mallarmé's "L'Après-Midi d'un Faune," who dreams the same dream, and who was a major influence on Faulkner's early poetry: his own "L'Après-Midi d'un Faune," and *The Marble Faun* are obvious and direct descendants. One very interesting two-page fragment of a mostly unpublished poem, among Faulkner's papers at the University of Texas, indicates that Faulkner at one time planned to introduce into *The Marble Faun*, or at least into an early form of the poem that was to become *The Marble Faun*, a character much like the "Shade of Pierrot," a sensual human "lover" to stand in direct complement to the rife fecundity of the nature around him, and therefore in direct contrast to the statue's own lifelessness. He was apparently to represent to the faun the same thing that the "Shade" represents to the sleeping Pierrot, his own ideal of sexual vigor. The poem is narrated by a statue recognizably the marble faun, and eight lines of it were in fact published in *The Marble Faun*.[29] The lover's song (lines 18-39 below) appears in *The Marionettes* in its entirety (pp. 19-21), as part of Pierrot's song of seduction:

> Those cries, like scatt[ered silve]r sails,
> Spread across an azure sea.
> Her hands also caress me,
> My keen heart also does she dare;
> Plunging white fingers through my hair
> While flocks of shining pleiades
> Like ghostly Oceanides,
> Turning always through the skies,
> White feet mirrored in my eyes,
> Weave a snare about my brain
> Unbreakable by surge or strain.

---

[28] Millgate's phrase, p. 64.

[29] *The Marble Faun*, in *The Marble Faun and A Green Bough* (New York, 1968), p. 33; versions of lines 1-4 and lines 8-11 appear as part of the published work on this page. Also I have completed the fragmented first line by reference to the line as it is printed in *The Marble Faun*.

Introduction

The breathing dark stops suddenly,
Where one beneath a balcony
Masked, as his lute's trembling notes
Drift noiselessly like silver motes
In a moonbeam, breathes above,
A lover singing to his love:

Your little feet have crossed my heart,
        Love.

Your little white feet;
And I am a garden sprung beneath your footsteps.

You are a trembling pool,
        Love.
A breathless white pool;
And I am a flame that only you can quench.

Then we shall be one in the silence,
        Love.
The pool and the flame;
Till I am dead or you have become a flame.

Till you are a white delicate flame,
        Love.
A little slender flame
Drawing my hotter flame like will- o-
the- wisp in my garden.

But now you are white and narrow as a pool,
        Love,
And trembling cool.
Let me drown mysef between your breast points,
        Beloved.

So he sings. There is no bliss
In any mortal lover's kiss
For me, a stone, half beast, half god.
The world turns sadly in my heart,
Dumb and blind, that only knows
    [   ] burning of all winter snows. . . .

  Ultimately, Faulkner seems to have intended, in Pierrot, to synthe-
size both types: the Don Juan—Jurgen-like Pierrot, for all of his sexu-

ality, is no less sterile and life-denying than the impotent, faunlike Pierrot, and both are guilty of the same vain self-contemplation as Marietta. Indeed, Pierrot in his love song brings to specific point the thematic relationships among vanity, beauty, and death, when he calls Marietta a "pool" and invites himself to "drown," like Summer, narcissistically between her "breast points." Pierrot and Marietta, then, are two sides of the same narcissistic coin, sterile and moribund in their selfish insistence on living exclusively for their own satisfaction.

IV

Perhaps a word needs to be said, finally, about the title, which seems at first to be oversimple in its implication that men are the playthings of fate. If this is the case, *The Marionettes* is directly related to another unpublished and undated poem fragment, also at the University of Texas, entitled "Two Puppets in a Fifth Avenue Win[dow]":

> . . . Again he tautens, yellow, eternal [   ]
> Again the other beneath him, staring at not[hing?]
> Concentrates to the destiny that compels him [   ]
> That impossibly articulates his arms.
> Yellow he rises through pitiless jerking gradatio[ns?]
> Yellow his face, swung downward and snared by elec-
>   trics,
> Unchanged, bloodlessly flouts Isaac Newton.
> Terrifically they poise to a parting of palms.
>
> Then for a moment they hang there, gaudy and froze[n?]
> A Spurious gesture of passion and flouted laws;
> Till downward he swings in ludicrous surrender;
> And to that force compelling them, they pause
> And relaxed, forever above or below any laughter
> Their faces, forever blind, stare through the elec-
>   trics,
> Implacably through distorted transparence of window
> Superbly still and sinister, before them at nothing[.]

Introduction

> And you, who on the pavement forever pass,
> Obeying without question forces that ever compel y[ou]
> You pause: for a moment you, too, are [   ]
> [   ]rgan of sight without brain, a ge[   ]
>   to support it;

The abrupt shift of attention from the observed puppet to the observing humans suggests, clearly, that there are similarities between the humans and the puppets: the puppets controlled by strings, the humans by other "forces that . . . compel."

Unquestionably, Faulkner throughout his career was interested in the idea of fate, and in the image of men as puppets, particularly when they could be used to add classical and tragic dimensions to his work.[30] Yet to assume too readily that *The Marionettes* is purely fatalistic, even with the Spirit of Autumn's insistence, is to overlook the fundamental human dimension in the play: the viewpoint that posits, in the First Figure's sensitive and compassionate response to the returned Marietta, a moral scale against which each of the characters can be measured. It would also be to overlook what Faulkner said not quite two years later about Joseph Hergesheimer's novels: his characters are merely "puppets he has carved and clothed and painted," he wrote, and they are part of a "terrific world without motion or meaning." He particularly disliked *Linda Condon* because it

is not a novel. It is more like a lovely Byzantine frieze: a few unforgettable figures in silent arrested motion, forever beyond the reach of time and troubling the heart like music. His people are never actuated from within; they do not create life about them; they are like puppets assuming graceful but meaningless postures in answer to the author's compulsions, and holding these attitudes until he arranges their limbs again in other gestures as graceful and as meaningless.[31]

But the characters in *The Marionettes*, at least in their creator's apprentice manner, *do* create life about them, *are* actuated from within, and therefore are not puppets at all. The singing voice that Marietta hears, her reaction to it, and Pierrot's studied and deliberate dissipation are caused not by the "author's compulsions" but by what Faulkner

---

[30] Perhaps the most moving and intricately articulated image of this type is Judith Sutpen's impassioned description of people "trying to, having to, move your arms and legs with strings only the same strings are hitched to all the other arms and legs and the others all trying . . ." (*Absalom, Absalom!* [New York, 1936], p. 127).

[31] "Joseph Hergesheimer: Linda Condon—Cytherea—The Bright Shawl," *Early Prose and Poetry*, pp. 103, 101–2.

Introduction

described over a decade later as the "old gutful compulsions," a fine phrase loaded with significance for any discussion of fate and free will in Faulkner's works.[32]

The title, then, is metaphor: fate is, to Faulkner, consequence, the entangling accretion of actions and reactions to circumstance. To say this is not at all to say that there are no forces beyond man's control with which he must contend; of course there are, and to the extent that man is a victim of such forces that he cannot control he is a pitiable creature, a "puppet" indeed. But Faulkner knows that man is too frequently the victim of forces and compulsions that he *can* control, if he only would; thus Pierrot. To whatever extent Faulkner's characters talk of fate, to whatever extent they comfort themselves by placing the responsibility for their entanglements on the shoulders of a puppet master, the reader must keep both the character and the circumstance in the ever-present moral context in which Faulkner places them; and he must hold characters individually accountable for their sins. The gutful compulsions are human in origin, and whether they be pride, ambition, vanity, lechery, or whatever combination, they are ultimately a form of narcissism, which is simple selfishness: the concern with self to the exclusion of all meaningful human relationship, the distortion of human relationship in order to satisfy one's own needs and desires. And whether that selfishness take the form of Pierrot's sad and self-defeating dissipation or of Marietta's sterile peacocklike adoration of her own heavily decorated and artificial image, the moral results are the same: in the final drawing, the only one that adds content to the text, Pierrot stands staring at himself in a full-length mirror, rather like the narcissistic moon staring "blank face to blank face" at itself in the pond, the apparently dead body of Marietta lying, supine, on a couch at his feet.

[32] "Black Music," in *Doctor Martino and Other Stories* (New York, 1934), p. 263. It is worth noting that Wilfred Midgleston, the story's central character, becomes, for one evening, a faun—or, as he puts it, a "farn."

The Marionettes

The facsimile which follows is of the Virginia copy of the play, which is slightly enlarged, and is presented without the first two blank leaves, one signed by Ben Wasson, and the final two blank leaves.

THE MARIONETTES

A PLAY IN ONE ACT

BY
W. FAULKNER

FIRST EDITION   1920

PERSONS

Pierrot
Marietta
Shade of Pierrot
A Grey Figure
A Lilac Figure
Spirit of Autumn

The sky is a thin transparent blue, a very light blue merging into white with stars in regular order, and a full moon. At the back center is a marble colonnade, small in distance, against a regular black band of trees; on either side of it is the slim graceful silhouette of a single poplar tree. Both wings are closed by sections of wall covered with roses, motionless on the left wall is a peacock silhouetted against the moon. In the middle foreground is a pool and a fountain.

Pierrot is seated at right front in a fragile black chair beside a delicate table. His left arm is curved across the table top, his right, arm hangs beside him, and his head rests upon his curved arm, face toward front. He appears to be in a drunken sleep, there is a bottle and an overturned wine glass upon the table, a mandoline and a woman's slipper lie at his feet.

He does not change his position during the play. He is dressed in white and black. Flung across the chair back is a scarf of black and gold Chinese brocade.

Two figures, grey and lilac, appear from the pavillion and come to the front, moving in a slightly unnatural rythm.

First Figure — How still it is! The air does not stir, the air is like a candle flaming in a dusky colonnade.

Second Figure — The sky is like a blue candle flame, the sky is a curtain of thin blue silk, and the wind stirs it gently like a white hand.

First Figure — No, the sky does not stir, it is the hair before your face that the wind stirs like a pale hand. The sky its-self is still; see, the stars are like silver apples pasted on thin blue silk.

Second Figure — The stars are like gardenias before they turn brown from the heat of a human body, the sky is like thin blue silk stirring upon a living breast. Why does the sky stir like silk with breathing? It is like the covered breast of a woman kneeling between two candles, and the moon is a Roman coin suspended upon her breast.

First Figure — The moon is like a dismembered breast upon the floor of a silent sea, the moon is like the bloated face of a scorned woman who has drowned herself. How still it is!

Second Figure — It is not still. The twin poplars are not still; see, they sway in unison like two violin bows, they are like two blind virgins swaying before

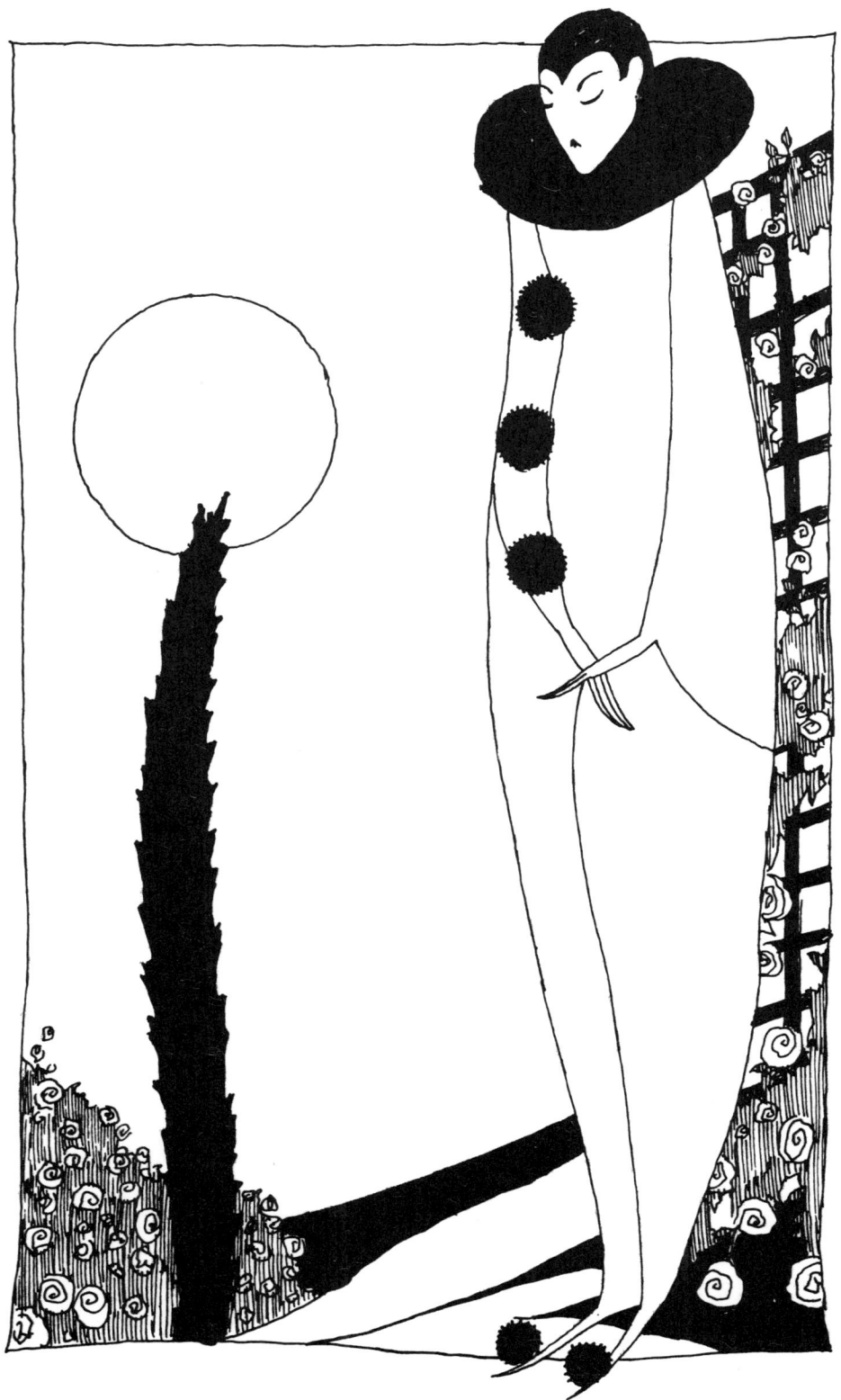

a colonnade, and the nine white columns of the colonnade are nine muses standing like votive candles before a blue mountain, they are nine candles flaming quiet circles on the ceiling of a marble pavilion where a young man, surrounded by slaves, lies sleeping, and the sky behind the pavilion is a curtain of purple velvet painted with stars in heavy gold. Do you not see how the sky sags with the weight of the stars?

First Figure — The twin poplars are like statues of virgins in dark green bronze, and their shadows are like reflections of two candles in a flat mirror. How still it is! There is no movement in this garden save the fireflies like blown sparks.

Second Figure — Hold, it is not still; someone is moving in this garden, the air is disturbed like ripples spreading across a still pond at dusk.

They withdraw behind the roses on the left wall as Marietta enters. She is dressed all in white and comes slowly to the front. She halts at the fountain, faces the moon and lifts her arms with a sudden gesture, lets them fall, and goes over to the rose bush at left and draws a great armful of them about her face. She then faces front, and all the time she is speaking she stands in a slightly strained but graceful attitude.

Marietta — I cannot sleep, my narrow bed is not cool tonight. My bed is heavy and hot with something that fills me with strange desires. Why am I filled with desire for vague, unnamed things because a singing voice disturbed my dreams? For I do not, I cannot, know the voice which sung beneath my window. No, no, I do not want to know, I am afraid to know! Am I afraid, I wonder? But my nightingales, they were afraid of the singing voice. The nightingales that once sung in my garden have flown; my garden is like a dark room when the candles are extinguished. Am I afraid of a darkened room? Ah, but it is something else; my bed has drawn sleep from my body as a stone wall absorbs the dew from the roses that cover it; my bed is like the breast of a peasant woman heated with labor in August vineyards, and the air in my room is shadowy with echoes like dying ripples, faint as the scent of honeysuckle at dusk. I cannot sleep in my room tonight. How still it is! There is no sound save that of the liquid gold nightingales, the liquid calls of the nightingales

ebb and flow upon my face with
faint sound, like tiny waves upon
a moonlit beach. How still it is!
and cool, but my face and my
body are not cool; my hands
are hot like magnolia petals at
noon, my body is hot like the
earth of a noon drenched garden. How cool the pool looks!
It is like a naked girl lying
on her back among the roses,
it is so cool that I shall
cool my face and my hot hands

in it. There is no one here, dare I bathe in this pool?

She approaches the pool as though undecided, then with a sudden movement, she slips off her gown and steps slowly into the water. She pauses, listening. There is a sound of voices from beyond the wall.

Voice — I am Pierrot, and was born
On a February morn

In Paris town, and on my head
The moon shone, weaving in my head
A spell, and 'till I am dead —
Chorus — And from then 'till we are dead
We have moon madness in the head,
We have moon madness in the head.
Voice — Every month, when comes the moon
I leave my musty garret room;
When she has cast her clothes a-
way,
To naked dream 'till break o' day —
Chorus — While she dreams the

night away
We play at love 'till break o' day,
We play at love 'till break o' day.

Voice — She calmly watches me below;
I am not calm, but to and fro
I sing and whirl and leaping dance,
Away all debt and toil I prance —
Chorus — We sing and whirl and leap-
ing dance
To mandolin's high dissonnance.

Voice — The roses nod to me and sigh,
The moon sits naked in the sky,

The cold is gone, 'tis month o' May,
I seek some one to come and play —
Chorus — We seek some one to come
and play,
Tomorrow is another day,
Tomorrow is another day.
Voice — My foster mother dreams above,
This night was made to sing and
love;
Your high shut garden tempted me,
Here's music for our revelry —
Chorus — Your high shut garden

tempted us,

O fair sweet maid, come dance with us —

O fair sweet maid, come dance with us!

The singing stops. Pierrot's head appears above the left wall, then he leaps up, and sitting tailor fashion upon the wall, strums his mandolin and sings,

Pierrot — Your little feet have crossed my
   heart,
      Love!
Your little white feet,
And now I am a garden sprung
beneath your footsteps.

But why do you tremble so,
      Love!
And your little hands are cold,
Your hands that have fallen like
plum petals within my garden.

You are a trembling pool,
    Love!
A breathless shivering pool,
And I am a flame that only you can
    quench.

Then we shall be one in the silence,
    Love!
The pool and the flame,
Till I am dead, or you have become
    a flame.

Till you are a white delicate flame,

Love!
A little slender flame,
Drawing my hotter flame like will-o-the-wisp in my garden.

But now you are white and narrow as
    a pool,
    Love!
And trembling cool.
Let me drown myself between your breast points,
    Beloved!

Marietta is frightened. As Pierrot leans toward her from the wall, she clasps her hands across her breast, watching him like one hypnotized.

Marietta — No, no, kind sir; I cannot dance!

I know not how, for my three aunts
Told me my mother went this way,
Slipped from her bed at break o' day
Because a strange voice sung to her,
Beneath her window on a night
Like this, blue velvet and moonlight,

[She was scarce as old as I]
Then she returned, my mother sweet,
And slow and sad were her white feet;
Yet slower still, till from her grave
There sprang a flower, sweet and brave
— The flower was I, so say my aunts
And I must never learn to dance.
O, please dont make me want to try!
Pierrot — Come, sweet maid, with me
        and dance.
Well I know your three grey aunts!
Three drab grey moths stirring about
A candle till the flame goes out.

Ah, would you have the flame go out?

    Slowly, step by step, as though in a trance, Marietta approaches the wall. Her hands are clasped upon her breast, her eyes are fastened upon Pierrot, she is like a sleep walker while Pierrot continues to sing, weaving his song like a net about her.

Pierrot — Come, love! Leave these roses sleeping,

From the poppies fairy sprites are peeping,
And on the sweet lawn myriad elves are dancing.
Come, let this tale be told
By my lute's throbbing gold
Growing like petals beneath the night entrancing.

Come, love! For the night is falling,
Within the wood where nightingales are calling:

— Come, ye lovers, come without regretting
Come, all the far world lies
A stage for our revelries.
Come, heart of my heart, to the garden of forgetting.

    Marietta has now reached the wall. Pierrot reaches down suddenly, and lifts her up. They stand erect upon the wall for a moment, a single black silhouette against the moon, then are gone. Pierrot's voice is heard, growing steadily fainter.

Pierrot — My foster mother in the sky
See my bright limbs flashing by!
I shake my hair, I stamp my feet,
And this maiden, grave and sweet,
This slender maiden, shivery white:
A rosebud shaken by moonlight!
Plunge your fingers in her hair,
Spin and weave moon madness there,
Spin your dreams within her head
And let them dance in her white bed
Till all her dreams are fever hot,
Rout peace until she knows it not;
But only madness in the head,

Desire to follow where I lead
While nightingales in every bush
Sing for my ear, and when I wish,
Strew silver sequins to enhance
My mandolin's high dissonnance.

    The voices slowly die away,
the moon disappears behind a cloud,
leaving the stage in darkness. The
grey and lilac figures can be dimly seen among the roses. There
is a sound like wind in the trees
for a moment, which, on dying a-

way, dissolves into the low tones of a violin.

First Figure — It is sudden cold. Do you feel how cold it is become? The wind is very chill, it draws harp like through the branches, it moans like a blind man seeking for a treasure, the wind is like a dead man seeking his friend —— Ah! what was that? A leaf: it is a dead leaf. There, another one. The trees are dying, for it is autumn; the Spirit of Autumn is somewhere in this garden, do you not hear his violin? The falling leaves are very heavy upon my face and my hands. Second Figure — Yes, the leaves are dying. All things must die, and dead things are very heavy.

The moon appears again. The spirit of Autumn is revealed sitting upon the right hand wall, playing a violin. He is dressed in deep purple, his face is downcast and indistinct. He continues to play while he is speaking, an occasional leaf falls slowly.

Spirit of Autumn — I see a garden of crimson roses and carven marble, and the songs of nightingales are woven about it like cloth of gold. Yet the roses in the garden stir voicelessly, for the Summer has gone, as is the way of youth, striding along the soft dim sky; his young flushed face is lifted and his head is bound with lilac stalks. And the garden nymph, from behind her screen of fading roses, watches him, as is also the way of youth. She leans her breast upon the balustrade, her breasts are like two birds in the shadow of her hair; her long fair hair hangs down and the moon is combed through it like spun silver. They have not quarrelled, I am sure the have not quarrelled, yet she is sad, she is filled with a foreboding of disaster; and because she is troubled by vague fears she sends her heart after him across the sweet pagan

heartbreak of the September night:
    Never the nightingale
        Oh my dear,
    Never again the lark
        Wilt thou hear.
Though dusk and the morning still
Tap at thy window sill;
Though ever love call and call
Thou wilt not hear at all,
    My dear, my dear!

Her voice reaches him, faint and fair and far as her own dying roses, yet he hears her, and he stops against the sky; perhaps his heart, too, misgives him. And so he stops, half turned toward her and for a fleeting second he is the utter master of his soul; Fate and the gods stand aloof, watching him, his destiny waits wordless on either hand. Will he turn back where she awaits him in her rose bower, or will he go on? Ah, he goes on, his young eyes ever before him, looking into the implacable fu‐ ture. Perhaps a newer, stronger love has called him away, perhaps he is fallen upon by wild beasts while traversing a dark forest, or perhaps, while crossing a stream, he slipped and was drowned. Yet she, among her dried rose stalks, waits for him to come along the sky; she waits in vain. There was none to fly to her when he fell, only the ripples of his fall to whisper across the pool, to be snuffed out like candles among the bordering reeds; the reeds that bow over the pool in a sudden rush of sorrow to watch him, beautiful in slumber.

She does not sing to him at all and the wind has whirled the refrain of her song away, for her warning of disaster had been a true warning, the disaster had come to pass, for truly:

> Though ever love call and call
> He will not hear at all,

no matter what faces bend above him or what mouths sing to his unheeding ears. While the half moon in the sky is forever staring blank face to blank face with the half moon in the stream.

The voice falls, and slowly the violin bow ceases to move, and the Spirit of Autumn sits silently upon the wall, lending a wordless brooding peace to the garden. He supplies a background in a single tone against which the succeeding action takes place, like a veiled mirror. Without moving or speaking he dominates the whole scene.

First Figure — It is autumn. The autumn will strip this garden, but the garden itself will not change. This garden is old, it has felt the chill of a thousand winters. But all things must grow old, we grow old alone; the earth is already old, the earth is like an aged woman gathering fagots in a barren field. Soon quiet snow will streak the earth with tears, but there are no tears in the earth's eyes now, she is blind with things that she has seen. There are no more gape mouthed crocuses and poppies wide with woe to wreathe her fingers; the earth is a hunched and sightless woman holding herself together with her hair.

Second Figure — Hither come the ghosts of stripped springs grown cold and dumb and sightless, and here come also winds from the blue Ionic hills over which the sunlight spills its muted gold, yet the hills are bare of any life, the fearful sheep gather in fold against the winter, subtle as a beast, and keen and cold.

First Figure — The trees shake their arms against the sky with light thin sound, the passing days scatter like petals on the ground as quietly as shattered roses, like sweet and sad and endless repetition of a name. The birds are gone, no birds here call and cry because of the cold, and the pool is grey like the sliding sky, the hair of the sky drifts grey across the pool, that lies like a hand with fingers slightly curled, holding all the muted world within its palm. Second Figure — The statues in this garden are not cold; they are all head. The leaves shake from the blond boughs and slide down the sky hill, and the moon, even the moon is a dead leaf blown across the sky. . . . Listen!

They conceal themselves again

as Marietta enters. She comes to the front looking about her as if she had never seen the garden before. She wears a flame colored gown.

Marietta — How this garden has changed! Why has it changed so? Ah, I know, it is autumn that has changed the garden, But I am not changed. Am I changed very much, I wonder?

She goes to the pool and

stares in it, turning her head this way and that.

First Figure — She has returned! Has Pierrot, then deserted her, has he left her for someone else? It is always someone else with him. Why do we fly to do his bidding, we who know him for the white sensual animal he is? For where goes Pierrot, also goes unhappiness for someone.
Second Figure — The more fools we.

First Figure — Yes . . . yes. The more fools we.

Second Figure — The more fools we.

Marietta [studying her reflection] No, I have not changed, I am really beautiful now.

Second Figure — How beautiful she is! She is like an ivory tower builded by black slaves, and surrounded by flames, she is like a little statue of ivory and silver for which blood has been spilt.

First Figure — She is like a slender birch tree stripped by a storm, she is a birch tree shivering at dawn upon a dim wood; no, she is like a young poplar between a white river and a road.

Second Figure — Her hair is gold, it is as gold as a galleon captured by pirates, gold bleachened with blood and passion; her hair is like a panther's flank at night.

First Figure — No, her hair is not gold, her hair is like the sun upon a field of wheat, it is like sunlight combed through maple leaves, and her eyes are like pools in the depths of a forest at night, like twin pools in which are caught scraps of evening sky; her eyes are like windflowers sown across a meadow.

Second figure — Yes, her eyes are like pools in which one could drown oneself, her breast is a narrow white pool, and her breast points are the twin reflections of stars. Her breasts are like ivory crusted jewels for which men have died, for which armies have slain one another and brother has has murdered

brother.

First Figure — Her breasts are white roses asleep upon a pool, and her breathing stirs her breast like the wind within a bed of roses; her breasts are like two white birds after a long flight. How beautiful she is!

Second Figure — How beautiful she is?

Marietta — No, I am not changed, but how my garden is changed! The leaves fall without sound and lie like wearied hands upon the pool. The leaves are dead, like hands that have held love, they are like the hands of those who have seen happiness before them, and when they reached out to touch it, found that their hands were like dead leaves palm upward upon a pool; the bare trees lean above the dead leaves like sorrowing faces. But my hands are not dead leaves, my hands are still beautiful.

First Figure — How beautiful her hands are! Her hands are like little fluttering white birds, her hands are like butterflies spreading their wings in the light and shade.

Second Figure — Her hands are two links of silver chain with which a slave has been shackled, they are like little pieces of smoothe silver for which lives have been bartered. How beautiful she is? Why is she so sad?

Marietta — One grows old, beauty goes as the leaves slip earthward in autumn, without any sound. I too shall grow old, but I am beautiful now. Nothing save death is as beautiful as I am, and I shall wear a jade gown, and walk on the gravel paths in my garden. When I walk the green motion of my gown will be repeated upon the jade on my finger nails, and my hair will be heavy with gold so that the weight of my hair will hurt my head. My temples will be smooth with gold also, and the gravel of the gravel path in my formal garden will hurt my feet; between the pains in my head and the slight pains in my feet will be jewels, and silver and dull gold chased cunningly by an Italian dying of tuberculosis, and the purple on my feet will be thick with rubies to rival the red points of my peacocks' eyes like the eyes of wolves upon a wood's edge. My peacocks are white smeared with purple and cry to their reflections in the bottomless pool below the cypress trees. And the lilacs beside the pool stare unceasingly at the lilacs within the pool until

the peacocks' cries shudder through them,
then the lilacs beside the pool stir, and
cry soundlessly to the lilacs within the
pool. And the cypress trees struggle upward from the pool and brush the stars
down into the garden.

I desire — what do I desire?

The wind smooths the sky's hair
smoothly back;

The wind combs the pines from grey
to black, while the cacophonous cries of
my peacocks shiver the ilex before the

statue of Hermes.

The ilex is grey, from a white island in a sea of amethyst, then a wind stiff with the voices of subterranean things streaked the sea with lapis-lazuli and faded the ilex gray; the ilex is grey as a grey wall and the white statue of Hermes is an island in a sea of ink, and the wind combs the sky from grey to black.

I shall sit on a grey wall, and I shall swing my painted legs

through intricate figures, and my breasts,
like twin moons that have been dead
for a thousand years, will stare heavily over my girdle of dull brass into
the garden where the moon streaks
the shadow hair with silver; and my
peacocks will follow me in voluptuous
precision, brushing the moonlight
from the path with their heavy
wings. Their eyes will grow avid
and thick and remorseless as
the eyes of virgins growing old,

and they will approach and eat the
jewels from my feet and the jade
clasps from my finger tips, and my
heavy hair and the gilded eyelids on
my eyes will attract them while
their cold feet mark my body with
thin crosses.

    I desire — what do I desire?
    The wind streaks the moon's
hair on the sky,
    The moon will play my body
when I die, and the cacophonous

cries of my peacocks have blighted the ilex before the statue of Hermes.

Curtain

Textual Appendixes

Textual Appendixes

Introduction

VERY LITTLE is known about the writing of *The Marionettes*. Without any documentation, Joseph Blotner places its completion in late December 1920.[1] Surely it is possible that Faulkner had written all or at least parts of it much earlier than that, since it bears so many and obvious relationships to the poetry he had by that time been writing for several years. But the inspiration for writing a play, and for its title, does seem to be associated with the founding of, and Faulkner's active membership in, The Marionettes, a University of Mississippi theatrical group, in September of that year, and so there is no real reason to doubt that it was written some time during the fall semester of 1920.[2]

There is, however, some uncertainty as to how many copies of the play Faulkner actually made. According to his own statement over a decade later, he "made and bound 6 copies by hand"; but his memory may not have been serving him well, since he also claimed that he "signed none of them" when in fact he signed (that is, gave his name on the title page) the four copies now known to have survived. "It was long ago and I dont remember," he wrote.[3] Ben Wasson, a fellow member of The Marionettes, recalls that when Faulkner showed him

---

[1] *Faulkner: A Biography* (New York, 1974), see "Chronology," p. 218 (notes).

[2] Blotner, pp. 283 ff. One critic has argued, on what seems to me very slim evidence, that the characters, plot, and physical format of Edna St. Vincent Millay's *Aria da Capo*, which Faulkner reviewed in the *Mississippian* a little over a year later (*Early Prose and Poetry*, pp. 84-85) bear such a close resemblance to *The Marionettes* that Faulkner must have seen it before writing and designing his own pierrot play and that *The Marionettes* must therefore date from 1922 rather than 1920, despite Faulkner's own date of 1920 on two of the four known copies. See James E. Kibler, "William Faulkner and Provincetown Drama, 1920-1922," *Mississippi Quarterly*, 22 (1969), 233-35, and my discussion of his evidence in "William Faulkner's *Marionettes*," *Mississippi Quarterly*, 26 (1973), 252-54.

[3] Meriwether, p. 9. Raymond Green wrote to Faulkner on 9 February 1932, requesting confirmation of his authorship. Faulkner wrote his reply at the bottom of Green's letter: "I wrote a play by that name once. It was never printed. I made and bound 6 copies by hand. I signed none of them. There may also be a mss. It was long ago and I dont remember."

Introduction

what was apparently the first copy of the play, he, Wasson, suggested that they might be able to sell a number of other copies. Faulkner authorized him to try, Wasson said, so that he could buy some whiskey. Wasson "sold five copies when [Faulkner] completed them, one copy at a time, one sale at a time. The price I received for each copy was $5.00. . . . In all, I had collected and given him $25.00 for the five copies I sold." Later, according to Wasson, Faulkner gave him "another copy" for acting as agent in the sale of the others.[4] If by "*another* copy" Wasson means a copy other than the first one he had seen; if the first copy was not one of the five he sold; and if he is correct in remembering having sold five copies, then Faulkner obviously made seven instead of six copies. One of the Texas copies, however, bears a dedication to "Cho-Cho," the first child, Victoria, of Estelle Oldham Franklin, whom Faulkner had hoped to marry (and eventually did, of course); it hardly seems likely that Faulkner would have included this copy among those he gave to Wasson to sell. If this is not one of the six or seven copies Wasson handled, and it doesn't seem likely that it is (unless of course Faulkner got one of the sold copies back, and inscribed it some time later), then Faulkner could have made as many as eight copies of *The Marionettes*, rather than the six he remembered in 1932; if eight, perhaps more.

Four copies are known to have survived: two at the University of Texas, one, owned by Mr. Howard Duvall and Dr. Don Newcomb, of Oxford, Miss., held at the University of Mississippi Library, and one at the University of Virginia, reproduced in facsimile in this volume.[5] The Virginia copy, bearing Ben Wasson's signature on the front fly-

---

[4] Ben Wasson, *A Memory of Marionettes* (Oxford, Miss., 1975), p. vi. Wasson's *Memory* is a pamphlet published and boxed with the Yoknapatawpha Press facsimile of *Marionettes*.

[5] Though there is some confusion about the precise number of surviving copies. The final page number in the Virginia copy is 55; 51 in the others. Carvel Collins, in *Early Prose and Poetry*, p. 18, called attention to a copy with 53 "pages of hand-lettering." When I queried Professor Collins about this, he kindly and helpfully replied (11 Feb. 1976) that he was, in *Early Prose and Poetry*, describing one of the two known Texas copies, that in that number he had included the hand-lettered title page and the hand-lettered page of Persons, and that 53 was therefore the total number of "hand-lettered" pages, not the final page number. Barbara Izard and Clara Hieronymus, in *Requiem for a Nun: Onstage and Off* (Nashville, 1970), p. 135, claim to have examined *three* copies of *Marionettes* at Texas, one of which had "fifty-three pages of script and nine pen and ink drawings"; but when I began work on *Marionettes* in the spring of 1973, there were only two copies in the Humanities Research Center at Texas. I have not seen a copy whose final page is numbered 53.

leaf, is almost certainly the copy that Faulkner gave him as his agent's commission; and the differences between it and the other three copies suggest that this was the original pamphlet; it is clearly the earliest of the four known copies. This would of course mean that what Wasson thought was *another* copy was in fact the one Faulkner first showed him. For as the Historical Collation, below, indicates, the text of the Virginia copy is substantially different, in hundreds of major and minor particulars, from the texts of the other three copies, which are virtually identical to each other.

Faulkner obviously hand-lettered the first copy of *The Marionettes*—again, probably the Virginia copy—from a prior typescript or holograph text. Some time after the first copy had been made, though it is not now possible to determine whether it was before or after Wasson's suggestion that he might sell some additional copies, he decided it needed further work, and then probably made his revisions on that earlier manuscript or typescript. Apparently he made at least one of the other five to seven copies from this revised manuscript, and then probably, and rather mechanically, reproduced the remaining copies directly from one of the copies of the bound revised text. I have been unable to determine any order of priority among the Mississippi and the two Texas copies, or whether any two of them are derived from the third as a common source.

Faulkner learned from his work on the first copy approximately how many pages the combination of text and illustrations would require, and so was able to "cast off" more accurately in producing the others: thus the Mississippi and the two Texas copies are bound in one gathering, whereas the Virginia copy required two. Other things indicate that the production of the copies subsequent to the first was a rather mechanical procedure. They are almost line-by-line reproductions of one another, with only occasional minor textual variations among themselves; Faulkner even misnumbered page 22 in all three of the later copies, numbering it 24. And there are some signs of relative haste in the fact that the drawings in the Mississippi and Texas copies are much less detailed than those in the Virginia copy. Compare, for example, the drawing facing page 45 of this volume with the same drawing, facing page 32 in the Mississippi facsimile.

Introduction

TO "CHO-CHO,"

A TINY FLOWER OF THE FLAME, THE ETERNAL GESTURE CHRYSTALLIZED; THIS, A SHADOWY FUMBLING IN WINDY DARKNESS, IS MOST RESPECTFULLY TENDERED.

FIRST EDITION 1920

Dedication to "Cho-Cho" in Second Texas copy. Verso of title page.

Textual Appendixes

Drawing on p. [iii] of First Texas copy. Compare with drawing on p. [iii] of the Virginia copy.

Introduction

Drawing facing p. 1 of the First Texas copy. Compare with drawing facing p. 1 of the Virginia copy.

Textual Appendixes

from beyond the wall, and Marietta stops

listening.

Voice — I am Pierrot, and was born

On a February morn

In Paris town, and on my head

The moon shone, weaving in my head

A spell, and till I am dead —

Chorus — And from then till we are dead

We have moon madness in the head,

We have moon madness in the head.

Voice — Every month when comes the moon,

Page 13 of the First Texas copy. Compare with pp. 14–15 of the Virginia copy to see changes in format Faulkner made in the later copies.

Introduction

Drawing facing p. 32 of the First Texas copy. Compare with drawing facing p. 45 of the Virginia copy. Note extra detail and care taken with the drawing in the Virginia copy.

Descriptions of the Manuscripts

Virginia Copy

Title Page: THE MARIONETTES | A PLAY IN ONE ACT | BY | W. FAULKNER
Verso of Title Page: FIRST EDITION 1920
Collation: [1]^{32} [2]^{10}. *Note:* Rebound and very difficult to determine. There are clearly two signatures.
Pagination: [2 blank leaves]; [i]: title; [ii]: date; [iii]: list of 'Persons'; [iv-v]: blank; [vi]: drawing; 1-6: text; [1 leaf, drawing on verso]; 7-16: text; [2 conjugate leaves, drawing on verso of first, recto of second]; 17-26: text; [1 leaf, drawing on recto]; 27-32: text; [1 leaf, drawing on recto]; 33-43, 43-45 [*sic*: 2 pp. numbered 43]: text; [1 leaf, drawing on recto]; 46-53: text; [1 leaf, drawing on verso]; 54-55: text; [2 blank leaves].
Paper: Off-white wove; 20.9 × 13.9 cm.; .003 inch thick. Leaves 3, 17-21, 23, 25-27, 29-30, 32, 37-40, 42 watermarked: 'E [in box] | TRANSCRIPT BOND'.
Ink: Black.
Binding: Rebound, apparently with original boards. Endpapers marbled. Leather spine, stamped in gold: 'THE MARIONETTES - FAULKNER'.
Note: Signed 'Ben Wasson, Jr.' on first of two blank leaves at front. Wasson claims that he had it rebound by Brentano's in the early 1930s (*A Memory of Marionettes*, p. vii).

Mississippi Copy

Title Page: MARIONETTES | A PLAY IN ONE ACT | BY | W. FAULKNER
Verso: Blank.
Collation: [1]^{44}.
Pagination: [2 blank leaves]; [i]: title; [ii]: blank; [iii]: list of 'Persons';

Descriptions of the Manuscripts

[iv–v]: blank; [vi]: drawing; [vii–viii]: blank; 1–12: text; [1 leaf, drawing on verso]; 13–20: text; [1 leaf, drawing on verso]; 21, 24 [sic], 23–26: text; [2 conjugate leaves, drawings on verso of first, recto of second]; 27–32: text; [1 leaf, drawing on recto]; 33–40: text; [1 leaf, drawing on recto]; 41–46: text; [1 leaf, drawing on recto]; 47–51: text; [52]: drawing; [5 blank leaves].

Paper: Off-white wove; 21.6 × 13.7 cm.; .003 inch thick. Leaves 23, 41–44 bear the same watermark as the Virginia copy. Watermarked leaves and their conjugates have a slightly coarser texture than the others.

Ink: Black.

Binding: White cloth spine; white boards. To the front is pasted a piece of black paper which covers all but a white frame around the edges. At top of black paper is pasted a white label, lettered in black ink: 'MARIONETTES | BY | W. FAULKNER'.

First Texas Copy

Title Page: MARIONETTES | A PLAY IN ONE ACT | BY | W. FAULKNER

Verso: Blank.

Collation: [1]^{42}.

Pagination: [2 blank leaves]; [i]: title; [ii]: blank; [iii]: list of 'Persons'; [iv–v]: blank; [vi]: drawing; 1–12: text; [1 leaf, drawing on verso]; 13–20: text; [1 leaf, drawing on verso]; 21, 24 [sic], 23–26: text; [2 conjugate leaves, drawings on verso of first, recto of second]; 27–32: text; [1 leaf, drawing on recto]; 35–40: text; [1 leaf, drawing on recto]; 41–46: text; [1 leaf, drawing on recto]; 47–51: text; [52]: drawing; [4 blank leaves].

Paper: Off-white wove; 21.2 × 13.7 cm.; .003 inch thick. Leaves 1–3, 6, 9–11, 21, 26, 31, 35–36, 38–39 bear same watermark as Virginia copy.

Ink: Black.

Binding: Same as Mississippi copy.

Textual Appendixes

Second Texas Copy

Title Page: MARIONETTES | A PLAY IN ONE ACT | BY | W. FAULKNER

Verso: TO "CHO-CHO," | A TINY FLOWER OF THE FLAME, THE | ETERNAL GESTURE CHRYSTALLIZED; | THIS, A SHADOWY FUMBLING IN | WINDY DARKNESS, IS MOST RE- | SPECTFULLY TENDERED. | FIRST EDITION 1920

Collation: [1]^{44}.

Pagination: [3 blank leaves]; [i]: title; [ii]: dedication and date; [iii]: list of 'Persons'; [iv–v]: blank; [vi]: drawing; 1–12: text; [1 leaf, drawing on verso]; 13–20: text; [1 leaf, drawing on verso]; 21, 24 [*sic*], 23–26: text; [2 conjugate leaves, drawings on verso of first, recto of second]; 27–32: text; [1 leaf, drawing on recto]; 33–40: text; [1 leaf, drawing on recto]; 41–46: text; [1 leaf, drawing on recto]; 47–51: text; [52]: drawing; [5 blank leaves].

Paper: Leaves 2–43 off-white wove; 21.5 × 14.0 cm.; .003 inch thick. Conjugate leaves 1 and 44, apparently used as some kind of wrapper, are made from a different paper, slightly heavier, whiter, and .004 inch thick. None of the leaves bears a watermark.

Ink: Black.

Binding: Same as Mississippi copy.

Historical Collation

HERE ARE LISTED all textual variants among the four known copies of *The Marionettes*, though it should be noted that many of the readings are listed with considerable uncertainty; it is frequently impossible to tell whether a punctuation mark is a period or a comma, a colon or a semicolon, whether a compound word has been written as one or two words; whether, for example, a word which is clearly "hypnotised" in the Virginia text (22.4) is "hypnotized" in the other three copies, or if what I've called a "z" is in fact one of Faulkner's backward *s*'s. When possible, I have solved such problems by reference to context; in other cases it has been necessary to choose one reading over another, and I have done so hoping to include problems and thereby call attention to them, rather than to exclude them.

Page and line numbers in the left column are keyed to the Virginia copy, reproduced in this volume, and the first entry is the reading of the Virginia text. Readings following the bracket or brackets are those in the other three copies, specified by the following symbols: X—Mississippi copy, Y—First Texas copy, Z—Second Texas copy, the one inscribed to Cho–Cho. Where all three of these texts agree with each other against the Virginia text, I have used no symbol, as in the entry for 1.5. The entry for 1.6 means that Y and Z are at variance with the Virginia text, but that X is not. Where the variant is *only* a punctuation mark I have used the curled dash (~) to show that the locating word on the line is the same in all denoted texts, and an inferior caret (ˬ) to indicate the lack of punctuation: thus the entry for 4.7 means that in the Virginia text there is a comma after the word "silk," but not in any of the other copies. Faulkner, here and throughout his career, inconsistently crossed *t*'s and *f*'s; I have not noted such irregularities except to prevent confusion. I have not noted Faulkner's changes in format for the lyrics. Entries for the second (and misnumbered) page 43 of the Virginia text are preceded in the left column by an asterisk (*). Explanatory remarks are in italics.

Textual Appendixes

Title	THE MARIONETTES] MARIONETTES
1.1	thin.] XZ˜,
1.2	light blue.] XZ˜˜,
1.3	white.] ˜,
1.5	colonnade,] pavillion,
1.6	distance,] YZ˜.
1.7	trees;] Z˜,
1.7-9	side of it is the slim graceful silhouette of a single poplar tree.] side is a slender poplar tree in graceful silhouette.
1.11	roses,]˜;
1.12-13	peacock silhouetted against the moon.] peacock, black against the lighter sky.
2.1	fore ground] Z foreground
2.1	pool.] XZ˜,
2.2-3	*extra space between these two lines*] no extra space
2.4	front.] Y˜,
2.7-8	beside him,] X at his side] YZ at his side,
2.11	sleep, there] sleep. There
2.12	overtunned] overturned
2.12	wine glass] XY wineglass
2.13	mandoline] mandolin
3.1-6	He does not change his position during the play. He is dressed in white and black. Flung across the chair back is a scarf of black and gold Chinese brocade.] He is dressed in white and black, flung across the chair is a scarf of black and gold Chinese brocade. He does not move during the play.
3.8	lilac,] X˜.
4.7	thin.] X˜,
4.7	silk,] ˜.
4.8	gently like] like
4.13-5.1	its- / self] XZ it- / self] Y its- / elf
5.1	still; see,] X˜, ˜.] Z˜; ˜.

Historical Collation

5.2	apples.] X~,
5.3–4	*no extra space*] XY *extra space*
5.7	body,] YZ ~;
5.13–6.1	Roman] flat Roman
6.1	coin.] ~.
6.7	her self] herself
6.9–10	still. The] X still, The
6.10–11	still; see,
	] X ~, ~;
	] Z ~, ~,
7.1	a.] Z a-
7.1	colonnade,] Z~.
7.4	before] around
7.6–7	marble pavilion where a young man,
	] XY pavillion in which a youth
	] Z marble pavillion in which a youth,
7.9–10	pavilion] pavillion
8.4	bronze,] ~.
8.5	reflections] the reflections
8.10	Hold,] Y ~;
8.11	still;] ~,
8.12	like] as with
9.1	pond] pool
9.2	with draw] withdraw
9.5	all in white] in white,
9.6–7	front. She halts at the fountain,
	] front, pausing at the fountain. She
9.7	lifts] raises
9.8	sudden] quick
9.9	fall, and goes over] fall and goes
9.10	rose bush] XZ rosebush
9.10	left.] YZ~,
9.11	a great] an
10.1–2	front, and all the time she is speaking she stands
	] the front and speaks, standing
10.3	strained.] XZ ~,
10.6–10	heavy and hot with something that fills me with strange desires. Why am I filled with desire for vague, unnamed things because
	] X no longer comfortable, it has filled me with strange

Textual Appendixes

        desires for vague, unnamed things. Why cannot I sleep tonight? Is it because
        ] Y *like X except:* desires,
        ] Z *like X except:* vague˄

10.11	dreams? For] Y dream? But
10.12	not, I cannot,] not know, I cannot
11.1	sung] sang
11.3	know,
	] X ˜˄
	] Y ˜!
11.3	I am] Y am
11.5	were] are
11.7	sung] Y sang
11.8	flown;] ˜,
11.9	dark room] room
11.11	Ah] Y Oh
11.12	else;
	] Y ˜:
	] Z ˜,
12.1	absorbs the] draws
12.3	it; my
	] XY it. My
	] Z it, my
12.4	woman.] XZ ˜,
12.4	heated] Z healed
12.8	honeysuckle] XY honey suckle
12.10	is!] X ˜.
12.11	save that of] save
12.12	nightingales,] XY ˜;
13.1	upon] across
13.2	faint.] Y ˜,
13.2	sound,] ˜˄
13.4–5	my face and my body are not cool;
	] XZ I am not cool,
	] Y I am not cool, and
13.6	like] as
13.7	noon,
	] X noon. and
	] Y noon and
	] Z noon, and

93

13.7	hot.] XZ~,
13.8	of] Y in
13.8	noon] sun
13.10–11	lying on her back] lying
13.11	roses,] ~;
13.13	hot hands] hands
14.3–5	pool as though undecided, then with a sudden movement, she slips off
	] X pool undecided, then, with a single movement, slips out of
	] Y pool undecided, then with a single movement she slips out of
	] Z pool, undecided, then, with a single movement, slips out of
14.7	water. She pauses, listening.] water.
14.9	wall.
	] XZ wall, and Marietta stops, listening.
	] Y wall, and Marietta stops listening.
14.10	Pierrot,] XZ ~.
14.11	morn.] X~,
15.3	and.] XZ ~,
15.3	'till] Y.~
15.4	'till] YZ.~
15.7	month,] ~.
15.8	moon.] ~,
15.9	room;
	] XZ ~,
	] Y ~.
15.10–11	away,] Y ~.
15.12	day—] ~.
16.1	away.] ~,
16.4	below;
	] X ~.
	] YZ ~.
16.6	and leaping] and leap and
16.6	dance,] Y ~.
16.7	debt] debts
16.8–9	and leaping] and leap and
16.10	To mandolin's high dissonnance.
	] X To mandolin's high dissonance,

Textual Appendixes

	To mandolin's high dissonance.
	] Y To mandolin's high dissonnance
	To mandolin's high dissonance.
	] Z To mandolin's high dissonnance,
	To mandolin's high dissonnance.
16.12	sigh,] XY ~.
17.1	'tis] XY ˏ~
17.1	May,] YZ ~ˏ
17.2	some one] Z someone
17.2	play—] ~.
17.3	some one] X someone
17.4	play,
	] X ~.
	] Z ~ˏ
17.7–8	above,] Y ~.
17.10	love;] ~,
17.11	me] us
17.12	Here's] YZ Heres
18.2	maid,] X ~ˏ
18.3	us—] ~,
18.4	maid,] XY ~ˏ
18.7	left wall] wall at left
18.9	upon] on
18.10	sings,
	] X ~:
	] Y ~.
19.2	heart,] X ~ˏ
19.11	within] in
20.3	breathless] little
20.6	shall] will
20.9	ˏTill] XY '~
20.9	dead,] ~ˏ
20.9	become
	] X beˏ/ come
	] YZ be- / come
20.11	ˏTill] XY '~
21.8	trembling cool.] cool.
21.11	Beloved!] XY ~.
22.3	across] upon
22.4	hypnotised.] hypnotized.

Historical Collation

22.5	sir;] ~,
22.9	bed] room
22.9	o'] of
22.10	strange voice sung to her,] stranger sang to her
22.11	window.] XZ ~,
22.12	moonlight,] ~.
23.2	returned] Z returnd
23.3	feet;
	] XZ ~.
	] Y ~,
23.4	till] and
23.4	grave.
	] X ~.
	] Y ~,
23.5–6	brave / —The
	] brave. / The
23.6	aunts.] ~,
23.8	O,] ~.
23.10	dance.] ~,
23.11	aunts!
	] XZ ~.
	] Y ~,
23.13	.till] '~
23.13	out,] XZ ~.
24.2	by step,] Z ~~.
24.2	though] though she were
24.4	upon] at
24.6	upon] on
24.6	Pierrot,] Y ~;
24.7	while] as
24.10	Come,] X ~.
25.1–2	peeping,] X ~.
25.4	dancing.] Z ~.
25.5	Come,] X ~.
25.6	By] In
25.6	lute's] X lutes
25.6	gold.] ~,
25.8	entrancing.] ~.
25.8–9	*extra space*] Y *no extra space*
25.9	Come,] XY ~.

Textual Appendixes

25.9	For] Now
25.9–10	falling,] XY ~˷
25.11	wood˷] Z ~,
25.12	calling:
	] X ~.
	] YZ ~˷
26.1	—Come, ye lovers,
	] X —.Hasten lovers
	] Y —Hasten, lovers,
	] Z —Hasten lovers,
26.1	regretting˷] ~—
26.2	lies˷] Z ~,
26.3	revelries.] Y ~,
26.4	Come,] X ~˷
26.4–5	garden
	] X gar˷/den
	] Z gar-/den
26.6	has now] has
26.7	reaches] leans
26.7	suddenly,] ~˷
26.9	for] Y far
26.10	silhouette against] shadow on
26.11	Pierrot's] YZ Pierrots
26.12–27.1	*no extra space*] *extra space*
27.1	sky˷] ~,
27.4	sweet,] Z ~˷
27.5	slender] Z shivery
27.5	white:
	] X ~˷
	] YZ ~,
27.6	rosebud˷] Z ~,
27.7	Plunge] Twist
27.7	hair,] ~˷
27.8	mAdness] madness
27.9	head˷] Z ~,
27.11	˷Till] XZ '~
27.11	hot,] X ~.
27.12	not;] ~,
27.13	head,] Z ~.
28.1–3	Desire to follow where I lead

97

Historical Collation

        While nightingales in every bush
        Sing for my ear, and when I wish,
        ] XY Desire to follow where I lead,
            And dance and dance if so I wish,
            While nightingales in every bush
        ] Z   Desire to follow where I lead
            And dance and dance if so I wish
            While nightingales in every bush

28.4	sequins.] Y ~,
28.6	voices slowly die] voice slowly dies
28.11–12	trees for a moment,
	] X trees
	] YZ trees,
29.3	cold. Do] cold, do
29.4	is] has
29.5–6	draws harp like through] is like a harp in
29.7–9	seeking for a treasure, the wind is like a dead man seeking his friend ———
	] seeking a friend ———
29.10	leaf: it
	] XY leaf, ... It
	] Z leaf, ... It
30.1	the Spirit
	] X The spirit
	] YZ the spirit
30.1	somewhere] XZ some where
30.2	garden,] Z ~;
30.7	very heavy] heavy
30.10	upon the right hand] on the right
30.11–12	is dressed in] wears a robe of
31.1	is speaking,
	] X speaks,
	] YZ speaks;
31.4	carven] carved
31.6	about] across
31.7	in the] in this
31.8	voicelessly, for the] voicelessly and die, for
31.9	gone, as is the way of youth,] gone,
31.10	soft.] Z ~,
31.10–11	sky; his young] sky, his

Textual Appendixes

32.2–3	him, as is also the way of youth.] him.
32.3	leans her breast] leans
32.4	balustrade,] ~;
32.5	hair;] hair, and
32.6	long.] YZ ~,
32.6	down.] XZ ~,
32.7	through] XY throug
32.8	quarrelled,] ~.
32.9	the] they
32.10	sad,] ~;
32.11	disaster; and.
	] X~, ~.
	] YZ ~, ~,
32.12	by] with
32.13	fears.] ~,
32.13	heart] Z heart out
32.14	him.] ~,
33.1	night:
	] XY ~.
	] Z ~.
33.2	nightingale.] X ~,
33.3	Oh.] ~,
33.5	hear,
	] X ~.
	] YZ ~.
33.7	sill;
	] X ~.
	] YZ ~,
33.8	and call.] X ~ ~,
33.13	her,] XY ~.
34.1	heart, too,] heart also
34.2	And so he] He
34.2	her.] ~,
34.3	second.] ~,
34.4	soul;] Y ~:
34.4	Fate] fate
34.5	aloof,] ~.
34.6	on either hand.] at his side.
34.8	Ah, he] He
34.9	young eyes] eyes

Historical Collation

34.11	Perhaps] Z Perhap
34.12	away,
	] XZ away, that he does not return;
	] Y away, that he does not return:
34.13	wild beasts
	] XZ beasts,
	] Y beasts
35.1	perhaps,] ~ ˏ
35.2	stream,] ~ ˏ
35.3	Yet] And
35.3	she,] Z ~ ˏ
35.4	stalks, waits] stalks waiting
35.4–5	to come along the sky;] to return to her,
35.8–9	pool, to be snuffed out like candles] pool and die
35.10	reeds; the reeds that
	] XZ reeds, only the reeds to
	] Y reeds; only the reeds to
35.11	sorrow
	] XZ grief
	] Y grief,
36.1	does not sing to him at all
	] sings no longer, she does not sing at all,
36.3	away, for her] away. Her
36.3–4	had been] was
36.6	ever love] XY love ever
36.6	and call.] ~ ~ ,
36.8	him.] ~ ,
36.10–11	is forever staring
	] XZ stares
	] Y stars
36.11	to blank face.] Y ~ ~ ~ ,
36.12–37.1	*no extra space*] *extra space*
37.2	Spirit] spirit
37.3	upon] on
37.4	wordless.] XY ~ ,
37.6	against] X a ˏ / gainst
37.7–8	place, like a veiled mirror.] place.
37.8–9	speaking.] ~ ,
38.1–2	change. This garden] change, for it
38.4–5	grow old alone; the] do not grow old alone. The

100

Textual Appendixes

38.6	gathering] Z gatheing
38.7–8	quiet snow] snow
38.8	the earth with tears,
	] XY her face with quiet tears;
	] Z her face with quiet tears,
38.10	now,] ~;
38.12	crocuses and] crocuses, or
39.1	wreathe] wreath
39.3	woman˄] ~,
39.5	come] comes
39.6	cold] old
39.8	also˄] ~,
39.8	the blue] blue
39.10	gold,] X ~;
40.4	light˄] ~,
40.8	repetition] repetitions
40.8	name.] Y ~;
40.10	cold,] ~;
41.1	sky,] ~;
41.2	that lies] lying
41.3–4	hold˄ / ing
	] XY holding
	] Z hold- / ing
41.4	muted] frozen
41.5	statues] X statue
41.5–6	gar˄ / den] garden
41.6	are not cold:
	] X not cold,
	] YZ are not cold,
41.7	boughs˄] X ~,
41.9	leaf˄] XY ~,
41.10	sky. . . .
	] X ~, ...
	] Y ~, ...
41.10–11	*extra space*] *no extra space*
42.1	front˄] Y ~,
42.6	Ah,] Y ~˄
42.6	il] I
42.7	autumn] the autumn
42.8	changed˄] Z ~,

101

Historical Collation

43.2–3	*extra space between these lines*] Y *no extra space*
43.4	Pierrot,] ~⌃
43.4	her, has] her? Has
43.5	someone] X some one
43.6	someone] X some one
43.10	someone.
	] X some one.
	] Y someone
43.10–11	*no extra space between these lines*] Y *extra space*
43.11	we.] Y ~⌃
*43.1	Yes . . .] ~. . . .
*43.1	yes. The] yes, the
*43.2	we.] ~!
*43.3	we.] ~!
*43.4	Marietta⌃] ~—
*43.4	have] am
*43.5	changed,] Y ~.
*43.5	beautiful⌃] X ~,
*43.8	slaves,] ~⌃
44.2	a dim] the dim border of a
44.2	wood;] Y ~,
44.2	no, she is like
	] XY no she is
	] Z no, she is
44.3	poplar⌃] X ~,
44.3	white river] XZ river
44.5	as gold as] like the gold of
44.6	bleachened] bleached
44.7–8	a panther's flank at night.
	] XZ the flank of a captured leopard.
	] Y the flank of a captive leopard.
44.9	No, her] Y Her
44.9	gold, her
	] X gold, he
	] Y gold. Her
44.10	upon] on
45.2	night,] ~;
45.3	sky;] ~,
45.3–4	like windflowers sown across a meadow.
	] XZ the color of wind flowers in the early spring.

102

Textual Appendixes

	] Y like two wind flowers in the early spring.
45.7	pool,] pool also,
45.8–9	the twin reflections of] like reflections of twin
45.9	are like] are
45.12	and] and for which
45.12	has has] has
46.3	pool,] Y ~.
46.4	within] in
46.5	roses; her] XY roses. Her
46.5	are like] are
46.8	is! [? *over* !]] ~:
46.10	is] XZ has
46.11–12	fall without sound and lie like wearied hands upon the pool. The leaves
	] fall, and lie on the pool like wearied hands. They
47.1–5	hands that have held love, they are like the hands of those who have seen happiness before them, and when they reached out to touch it, found that their hands were like dead leaves
	] the hands of one who has held love, like the hands of one who has tried to grasp happiness, and who finds that his hands have become dead leaves,
47.6	upon] on
47.6	pool;
	] XZ pool, while
	] Y pool. While
47.7	above the dead leaves] over the pool
47.12	Her hands] They
48.6–7	pieces of smoothe] smooth pieces of
48.8	is?] ~!
48.11	earthward in autumn,] earthward,
48.12	too.] X ~,
49.1	now. Nothing] now; nothing
49.2	am, and] Y am. And
49.3	jade gown, and walk on] gown of green jade, and I shall walk in
49.4	in my] of my formal
49.4	walk.] ~,
49.5–6	upon] by
49.7	gold.] ~,

Historical Collation

49.9	gold.] XZ ~,
49.10–11	path in my formal garden] paths
49.11	feet;] feet, and
49.12	pains] slight pain
50.1	pains] pain
50.1	jewels,] XZ ~.
50.2–3	chased cunningly] cunningly chased
50.5	rubies] jewels
50.6	peacocks' eyes
	] XZ peacock's eyes,
	] Y peacocks eyes,
50.8	white smeared with] white and
50.8	cry] they cry
50.9	therr] their
50.11–12	unceasingly] unstirringly
50.12	untit] until
51.1	peacocks' cries
	] XZ cries of the peacocks
	] Y cries of my peacocks
51.1	them,] ~;
51.2	the pool] Y the
51.5	pool and brush the
	] XY pool, and brush
	] Z pool and brush
51.7	what] What
51.8	smooths] Y smoothes
51.9	back;
	] XZ ~.
	] Y ~,
51.11	cacophonous] cacaphonous
51.12	shiver] shudder through
52.2	from] it came from
52.3–4	then a wind stiff with the voices of subterranean things] and a wind
52.5	lapis-lazuli] X lapiz-lazuli
52.6	gray; the] grey. The
52.7	as] like
52.7	white statue] statue
52.8	an] a marble
52.9	ink,] shadow,

Textual Appendixes

52.10	from grey to] grey and
52.11	wall,] XZ ~ ˬ
53.1	figures, and
	] XZ figures;
	] Y figures; and
53.6	and my] XZ my
53.10	wings] tails
53.11	remorseless as
	] X remorseless, as
	] Y remorseless, like
53.12	old,] XY ~;
54.2	feet ˬ] ~,
54.3	tips,] X ~ ˬ
54.4	hair ˬ] ~,
54.5	them ˬ] XZ ~,
54.8	what] What
54.9	moon's] Z moons
54.10	sky,] XZ ~.
54.12	die,] Z ~ ˬ
54.12	cacophonous] cacaphonous

Alterations in the Manuscripts

LISTED HERE are all significant alterations in each of the copies of *The Marionettes*. In addition to the symbols X, Y, and Z, used in the Historical Collation, the symbol V is used here to refer to the Virginia text. Page and line numbers in the left column are, again, keyed to the present volume.

5.11   Z the] *written over 'a'*
6.6   Y scorned] *'sc' written over undecipherable letter*
8.4   Y shadows] *first 's' written over undecipherable letter*
9.9   V goes] *'o' written over 'e'*
10.5   Y bed] *'e' partially blanked*
15.12   Y dream] *'r' written over 'e'*
17.3–4 Z someone] *Faulkner wrote 'somplay'; erased 'pl' and 'y', wrote 'e' over erased 'p', let 'a' stand for 'o', then wrote 'ne' over erased 'y'.*
21.10   X breast] *Faulkner started, but didn't complete, a final 's'*
26.7   Y leans] *'e' written over 'a'*
28.10   Y roses] *first 's' written over an 'e'*
41.1   Y sliding] *second 'i' written over 'e'*
41.6   X head] *'d' written over 'rt'*
*43.1   X First] *written over 'Yes'*
46.8   V is] *followed by '!' over '?' or vice versa*
49.9   V smooth] *unclear final letter blotted out, perhaps 'e'*